Elements of the Art of Architecture

Elements of

the Art of Architecture

WILLIAM MUSCHENHEIM

F. A. I. A.

Thames and Hudson · London

Contents

ACKNOWLEDGMENTS

The series of plates in the following pages were originally prepared with the assistance of a grant from the Horace H. Rackham School of Graduate Studies, University of Michigan.

Edward Hammarskjold, A.I.A., John M. Arms, A.I.A., and Turhan Beygo, as research assistants, contributed substantially toward the realization of this project. The impetus for this undertaking should be attributed to the members of the Committee on Education of the Detroit chapter of The American Institute of Architects.

I am indebted to the generous assistance extended by Mrs. Constance I. Sanchez, Mrs. Ruth E. Coghlan, and others of the library and staff of the College of Architecture and Design, as well as to Miss Eleanor S. Collins of the Department of Fine Arts, and to those in the main library at the University of Michigan.

In addition I wish to acknowledge the help of my wife, Harold Binder, A.I.A., the late Talmage C. Huges, F.A.I.A., Professor Robert C. Hutchcroft, Professor Robert L. Iglehart, Professor Herbert W. Johe, A.I.A., George P. Lenox, Dean Freeman Miller, Professor Walter B. Sanders, F.A.I.A., Dr. Ernst Voege, Dean Philip N. Youtz, F.A.I.A., and many others who assisted and encouraged me.

I also wish to express my appreciation to Mr. Bryan Holme, Miss Beatrice Trueblood, and Mr. Frank Platt of The Viking Press for their assistance and attention to the details of the publication of this book.

Foreword

The purpose of this book is to illustrate the essential qualities of the art of architecture and to stimulate an interest in them. Photographs of buildings created in periods and places from the great Greek civilization to present-day Europe and America have been selected and juxtaposed to show how specific characteristics as well as basic elements of design constantly reappear in different guises throughout the centuries.

In recent times there has been a particular emphasis on the functional aspects of architecture. Yet, although no building has sufficient reason for being unless it fulfills the everyday need for which it is designed, the quality of architecture as an *art* is of first importance from a cultural point of view, and most necessary if the interested participation of the layman is to be earned. It is with this in mind—the appreciation of the artistic aspects of architecture—that the book is presented—for laymen, practicing architects, and students.

The final form of an architect's design is dictated by the structural system and materials employed, by the purpose for which the building is to be constructed, and by its immediate environment, as well as by political, social, and economic forces. However, there are certain artistic qualities, exemplified in the best civic and domestic architecture of every period of Western culture, that have a universal validity, that transcend time, technology, locale, and climate as well as social and economic factors. For the most part, examples of these qualities have been chosen for demonstration purposes.

The scientific advances of the twentieth century have been so impressive that no human activity has escaped their influence. Our way of life has changed to the point that many of the basic values we used to accept now seem questionable to us or even outmoded. The technical, economic, and social factors that make the modern world have forced the issue of setting up new standards with, regrettably, a minimum of artistic, cultural, and spiritual direction. This is particularly noticeable in the field of building—or architecture, which is essentially the art of building. Many people have been overwhelmed by the scientific approach to the subject and question the validity of the term "architecture"; they feel that a scientifically developed environment would obviate any concern about architecture as an art. This attitude follows logically from a strictly utilitarian or materialistic point of view engendered by a highly industrialized and technologically advanced civilization. But for other people not all questions are answered in these terms; they search for qualities in architecture that go beyond a mere fulfillment of functional requirements for human activities and comforts, however important these requirements may be. For them, the important qualities in any art are those which skillfully interpret the aspirations of an epoch, whether toward harmony or the dynamically expressive, toward the rational or the mystical.

When intensively cultivated, the imaginative faculties of the artist can create harmonious relationships of line, mass, space, and color that have a universal appeal. However, the cultural climate of any period determines the degree of participation in the arts by laymen; that is, the extent to which new achievements are brought to the attention of the public and the readiness of the public, in turn, to accept new concepts of design and take an active interest in future developments. This factor is no less important than economic and political influences in the development of art and architecture. The cultural climate also determines aesthetic theory—the commonly accepted definitions of problems in aesthetics, of relationships among the arts, and of the role art and architecture are to play in any community. In our own century a conspicuous example of a world-wide movement was the part played by artists such as Kandinsky, Klee, and others on the staff of the Bauhaus when the significant work of that institution was being accomplished in the 1920s in Germany.

These problems, however, are cultural. It is evident that the keys to purely architectural expression are the character of the structural framework and the materials employed for the enveloping walls. Recognition of the special properties and limitations of whatever methods and materials are adapted to its purposes controls the development of an architectural design. The intense preoccupation of architects with these problems indicates a never-ending search for purer or more evocative solutions and combinations.

Throughout the book architectural qualities relating to form, space, and surface are illustrated, for it can be said that the most interesting and successful architectural work is almost always the result of a struggle on the part of the architect to interpret a contemporary way of life through the use of appropriate forms, spaces, and surfaces. These three elements of design are employed in his specifically trained—at times masterly—handling and composing of structural systems and materials (stone, concrete, metal, wood, stucco, glass, etc.,—whatever is, was, or will be available), and his integration of the functional, human, and social requirements of structures or groups of structures into a single whole. Harmony and the effective use of contrast are other qualities that contribute to a successful design. A building may be impressive, elegant, agreeable, poetic, or fantastic in form and may provide architectural spaces that are enjoyable, livable, or spiritually uplifting. Whatever its purpose, it should evoke in the beholder a sense of fulfillment.

Despite differences in the living standards, technology, culture, and other aspects of the various periods and countries to which the examples belong, the distinctly architectural qualities are recognizably related. The results show whether the designer is more concerned with problems of harmony and order or with what is sometimes termed an organic approach to design. The first method requires careful manipulation of mathematical or geometric proportions according to a strict system; the second emphasizes not the more recognizable mathematical and geometric proportions but a freer expression of the inner qualities of structural systems and materials; it permits a wider and more complex range of spatial development and the creation of incisive forms with composite interrelationships. These opposing tendencies can be traced throughout the history of Western architecture; sometimes one has been in the ascendancy, sometimes the other.

It is clear that the philosophic attitudes prevalent at any time have guided architects and artists in determining methods and goals. If we assume—for the sake of convenience—that Western culture began in Greece about 400 B.C., we can follow the changing patterns of thought in succeeding epochs as these patterns are mirrored in the architecture remaining in the Mediterranean area, in northern Europe, in the Americas, and in other parts of the world where Western influences have dominated. Oriental culture has been an important influence at times, but in this study we will concentrate on aspects of Western culture and the architectural characteristics that developed under its auspices.

Basic elements of architecture are illustrated as they occur in every type of building, whether ancient temple or modern industrial structure, elaborate palace or modest individual and community dwelling. A strict chronological division into architectural periods is not observed; instead, the similarities and contrasts of generally quite unrelated styles are compared here in an attempt to clarify what architectural elements are employed—and how—to produce harmony and a strong yet pleasing impact on the observer.

A synopsis of the principle characteristics of the various periods of architecture in the Western world is included for easy reference at the end of the book.

Elements of the Art of Architecture

Form

Three elements—form, space, and surface—are the essence of the art of architecture, and the following pages have been divided into three corresponding groups or chapters. In this first section the selections from different centuries demonstrate form.

In determining form, the principal concern of the architect is with the relative values of mass, volume, plane, line, solid, and void. Proportion, size, and scale are usually related to the human figure, but reference points in the environment, such as landscape, townscape, and sky, are often used. Light and shadow are also important in defining form.

Formal harmony is generally said to occur when a number of similar or related units are arranged in an orderly and unified composition that achieves a static balance. Formal contrast occurs when a tension between opposites is established, so that their polarity is clearly visible, or when one part of a building dominates another in a dynamic composition which can be expanded by development of rhythmical relationships. A vertical mass, for example, may contrast with a horizontal mass, or the special character of a plastic element may be emphasized by the contraposition of skeletal or planar members.

Pure cubical form geometrically subdivided with a deliberate emphasis on perfection of proportions and details

As a result of their attempt to find unity in multiplicity, the Greeks established mathematical principles of order. Their mathematical theories have been translated into rules of design which, together with their emphasis on precision in detail, have been followed in the architecture of various periods ever since the Greeks brought them to perfection about 400 B.C.

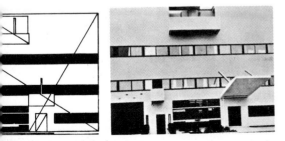

TOP LEFT: Petit Trianon: Versailles, France, 1769, Jacques Ange Gabriel, architect. (X Phot)
TOP RIGHT: Polygonal Wall: Delphi, Greece, c. 500 B.C.
BOTTOM LEFT: Athenian Treasury: Delphi, Greece, c. 400 B.C.
BOTTOM RIGHT: Weissenhof Housing: Stuttgart, Germany, 1927, Walter Gropius, Le Corbusier, Jacobus Johannes Pieter Oud, architects.
LEFT: Villa: Garches, France, 1927, Le Corbusier, architect. (Editions Girsberger)

15

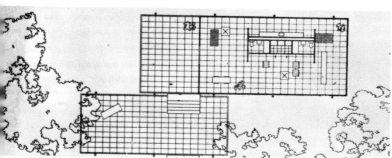

LEFT: Erechtheion: Athens, Greece, 393 B.C., Mnesicles, architect. (*Neue Photographische G.A.G., Berlin*)

RIGHT: Temple of Athena Nike: Athens, Greece, 427 B.C., Callicrates, architect. (*Alinari Art Reference Bureau*)

BELOW: "Bremo," Cocke House: Fluvanna County, Virginia, United States, 1815, Thomas Jefferson, architect. (*Wayne Andrews*)

BOTTOM AND PLAN LEFT: Farnsworth House: Plano, Illinois, United States, 1951, Ludwig Mies van der Rohe, architect. (*Hedrich-Blessing Studios*)

Porticos relating interior to exterior reflect an element of Greek humanism

The Greeks introduced the idea that buildings, like sculpture, can stand freely in space. This idea, and the actual relationship of Greek buildings to the open spaces around them, reflected the more liberal attitude toward life which resulted from the Greek interest in purely human experience and in a rational explanation of nature. It represented a rejection of the rigid and hieratic character of Egyptian art and architecture.

During the 18th and 19th centuries the rational outlook, as opposed to aspects of Christian theology, was expressed in architecture in a new type of classicism that recalled the clarity and comparative simplicity of Greek antiquity and its emphasis on the relationship of man to nature. This basic attitude, a heritage of Western culture, is mirrored in certain examples of contemporary architecture, but without the associational elements reminiscent of the architecture of the Golden Age in Greece.

17

Open colonnades and porticos spatially modulated by horizontal and vertical planes

From the Greek idea of designing buildings that were free-standing followed the recognition that the inner organization of a building helps to determine the outer form and to define clearly the contrasts between solid and void.

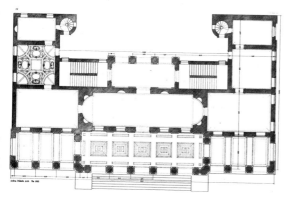

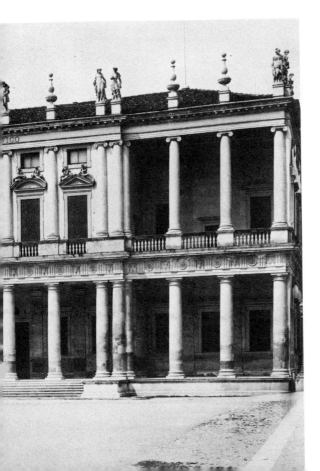

TOP: German Pavilion: Brussels, Belgium, 1958, Egon Eiermann and Sep Ruf, architects. (*Copyright: Platow's Kunstanstalt, Düsseldorf*)

FAR LEFT: Erechtheion: Athens, Greece, 393 B.C., Mnesicles, architect. (*M. Liffo, Athens*)

PLAN AND BOTTOM RIGHT: Palazzo Chieregati: Vicenza, Italy, 1550, Andrea Palladio, architect. (*Alinari Art Reference Bureau*)

19

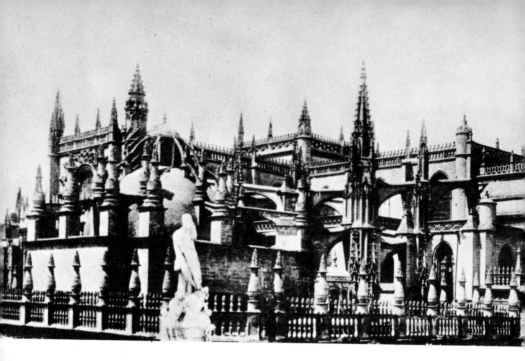

Exploded building masses expressing each element separately as opposed to the classical approach to design

The principles of design in the Middle Ages were not frozen into a limiting set of rules derived from concepts of harmony and proportion. The philosophy of the time was largely concerned with spiritual order, and in architecture this outlook resulted in a struggle to lighten the bodily structure of buildings and to emphasize directional arrangement.

In medieval work the directional emphasis was vertical—interpreted generally as symbolizing a quest for a higher truth. In modern work, when a dynamic quality in a building design is sought, the horizontal and the omnidirectional are stressed.

Palace of the Soviets: Moscow, U.S.S.R., 1941, Le Corbusier, architect. (*Lucien Hervé*)

ABOVE: Cathedral: Seville, Spain, 1402–1520, Isambret, Carlin, Rodriquez, and others, architects. (*Alberto Linares*)

Church of St. Étienne: Caen, France, 1065, Master Wilhelm, architect. (*Lévy et Neurdein Réunis, Paris*)

Cubical forms with arched openings and incidental domes

Between the Classical and medieval periods, when Christianity was emerging as the strongest spiritual and cultural force in the Western world, certain Oriental elements were mirrored in the buildings—especially in the Mediterranean area, where the Moslem influence, with its particular contributions in the field of geometry, also extended.

22

TOP LEFT: Trinita di Delia: Castelvetrano, Sicily, Italy, second half of 12th century. (*Coraddo Ricci*)
TOP RIGHT: S. Giovanni degli Eremiti: Palermo, Sicily, Italy, 1148.
BOTTOM LEFT: Chemical Factory: Lubań, Poland (formerly Germany), 1911, Hans Poelzig, architect.
BOTTOM RIGHT: Wainwright Tomb: St. Louis, Missouri, United States, 1892, Louis Sullivan, architect. (*Wayne Andrews*)

Directness in architecture at early stages in the development of various styles

Uncompromisingly straightforward, even blunt handling of architectural elements distinguishes work which is (comparatively) independent of inherited or outside influences. This is illustrated in the design of the early Romanesque cushion capital (*top left*), where the transition from the springing arch to an oblong plinth, to two square capitals, and finally, to two round columns occurs without hesitancy. The cantilevered control tower (*bottom left*), with its narrower base between the tracks exhibits a similar quality in its design.

Hohenstaufen Palace: Wimpfen, Germany, c. 1100.

TOP RIGHT: Monadnock Building: Chicago, Illinois, United States, 1891, Daniel H. Burnham and John W. Root, architects. (*Chicago Heritage Committee, photo by R. Nickel*)

BOTTOM RIGHT: Tramway Workers' Club: Moscow, U.S.S.R., 1929, K. C. Melnikov, architect.

LEFT: Yselmonde Railroad Signal Box: Utrecht, The Netherlands, c. 1930, S. van Ravesteyn, architect.

24

Steiner House: Vienna, Austria, 1910, Adolf Loos, architect.

S. Stefano: Bologna, Italy, 10th–12th centuries. (*Biagi and Zoboli, Bologna, Italy*)

Clearly defined
and articulated form

Architecture during the Romanesque period is distinguished by a certain bluntness and disdain for embellishment, probably related to a literal interpretation of religious asceticism. Even at an early date, however, there was an interest in composing rhythmical relationships of lines, forms, and masses whose original function was to subdivide, bound, and articulate one area in relation to another. This process of clarification and rationalization was one characteristic of the growth of scholasticism, which was to dominate the thought of the Middle Ages. A related intellectual attitude may be observed in early designs of the modern period.

TOP LEFT: Bauhaus: Dessau, Germany, 1926, Walter Gropius, architect.

TOP RIGHT: Church of San Vicente: Avila, Spain, c. 1200, Maestro Mateo, architect.

BOTTOM LEFT: Worms Cathedral: Worms, Germany, 1170–1230.

BOTTOM RIGHT: Turbinenfabrik-A.E.G.: Berlin, Germany, 1909, Peter Behrens, architect.

Fortifications: Aiguesmortes, France, 1275. (Photo CAP/© SPADEM, 1964 by French Reproduction Rights, Inc.)

Chrysler Corporation Truck Plant Export Building: Detroit, Michigan, United States, 1938, Albert Kahn, Inc., architects. (Hedrich-Blessing Studios)

I.I.T. Boiler Plant: Chicago, Illinois, United States, 1950, Ludwig Mies van der Rohe, architect.

Fort Saint-André, Entrance Gate: Villeneuve-lès-Avignon, France, mid-14th century. (*Photo CAP/© SPADEM, 1964 by French Reproduction Rights, Inc.*)

Forthright controlled and expansive forms in utilitarian structure

The scientific revolution of the 19th century produced a tendency to treat man and society in mechanistic terms. From this attitude the doctrine of utilitarianism emerged. The most distinctive characteristics of this kind of architecture are the large unbroken surfaces of glass, stone, or brick, against which other elements, such as doors, openings, skylights, turrets, chimneys, battlements, etc., appear in sharp and strong contrast. The contrast is further augmented by the fact that these elements occur either singly or far apart from one another. The texture of the large surfaces results from regard for and straightforward handling of the technical qualities of the materials, without the addition of any decorative components. Historically there has always been an engineering approach to certain types of structures designed for military or civic purposes and many interesting examples survive.

Vigorous, clear, and direct architectural design concurrent with social revolutions

When upheavals resulting from revolutions leave large voids in the culture as well as in the social structure there is room for bold experimentation in design. Deliberate rejection of the conventional standards of the old order releases exuberant creative impulses which seem to uncover new and more vibrant forms of expression in art and architecture. Inherited academic rules of design are to a large extent consciously discarded as lifeless. Audacious and original conceptions such as the design for the artisan's atelier (*center left*) appear. Interest shifts from subtleties and decorative detail to clear, even harsh statement of forms, color, and texture. The materials are used in a forceful and uncompromising manner which imparts a new, expressive quality to flat stucco surfaces, broad glass areas, and incidental steel elements such as stairs, rails, chimneys, etc. The resulting architectural character has influenced designs such as the one for the warehouse in Frankfurt am Main, (*center and bottom*) built in 1961, when a revolutionary or even a post-revolutionary situation was not in force. The criteria of design are oriented toward the deliberate achievement of the freshness and vitality that occurred in the historical examples.

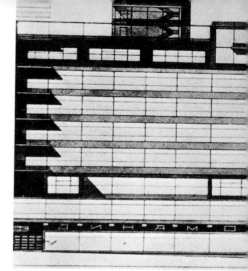

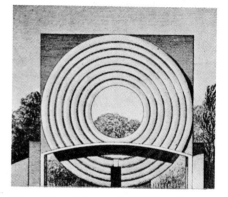

TOP LEFT: Maison O.G.P.N.: Moscow, U.S.S.R., 1926, J. A. Golosow, architect. (*Éditions Albert Morancé, Paris*)
TOP RIGHT: Hidekelclub: Leningrad, U.S.S.R., 1927, Kasimir Malvitsch, designer. (*Éditions Albert Morancé, Paris*)

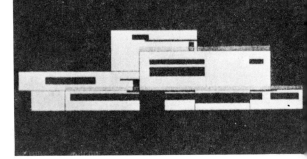

CENTER LEFT: Artisan's Atelier: France, c. 1800, Claude-Nicolas Ledoux, architect.
CENTER: Warehouse, Rooftop Court: Frankfurt am Main, Germany, 1961, Egon Eiermann, architect.

CENTER RIGHT: Salt Granary: Compiègne, France, 1783, Claude-Nicolas Ledoux, architect.
BOTTOM: Warehouse: Frankfurt am Main, Germany, 1961, Egon Eiermann, architect.

Vigorously shaped individual building elements ignore general principles of order

Disregard for architectural conventions may result less from planned opposition than from natural, unfettered human feeling for form, through which segments of buildings are shaped and related to each other in an organic, not a formalistic manner.

TOP LEFT: City Hall: Kurashiki, Japan, 1960, Kenzo Tange, architect. (*Ch. Hirayama*)

ABOVE: Village Hall: Saynatsalo, Finland, 1951, Alvar Aalto, architect. (*Eino Makinen*)

RIGHT: Haus zum Mittleren Pelikan: Zurich, Switzerland, 18th century. (*Photoglob-Wehrli AG*)

BELOW: Alte Hofhaltung: Bamberg, Germany, 16th century. (*J. H. Sf.*)

BOTTOM LEFT: Piazza Garibaldi: Bergamo, Italy, 1200–1400. (*Compagnia Fotocelere, Turin*)

33

Planes and openings dissimilar in shape and size in both Renaissance and Modern structures

An interesting and complicated balance results from the composition of elements in such a way that the modular system is neither simple nor especially apparent. The integration of large and small horizontal and vertical surfaces or openings into a totality is so executed that casual relationships of parts is the salient quality.

LEFT: Schröder House: Utrecht, The Netherlands, 1924, Eerrit Thomas Rietveld, architect.

FAR LEFT: Hôtel de Valois: Caen, France, c. 1550, Blaise de Plestre, architect. (*Photo CAP/© SPADEM, 1964 by French Reproduction Rights, Inc.*)

BELOW: Schlosshof in Alten Schloss: Stuttgart, Germany, 1553, Alberlin Tretsch, architect.

LEFT: Richards Medical Research Building: University of Pennsylvania, Philadelphia, Pennsylvania, United States, 1960, Louis Kahn, architect. (*Malcolm Smith*)

Both indigenous and sophisticated architecture blend effectively with the landscape.

Whether an organic approach to architectural design is conscious or unconscious, the results are similar. In the examples shown, the free plastic development of building forms is so closely related to the rugged, rocky character of the surrounding scenery that the buildings seem to be organic stratifications.

House: Pontresina, Switzerland, c. 1700. (B. Sommer, Samaden)

Church: Fextal, Switzerland, 17th century. (*B. Sommer, Samaden*)

Chapel: Ronchamp, France, 1955, Le Corbusier, architect. (*Lucien Hervé*)

Complex geometrical development in Islamic, Gothic, and Modern architecture

The intellectual and spiritual developments of the 13th and 14th centuries are illustrated in both the Islamic and the Gothic buildings of the time. Complex geometric number relationships were applied through specially developed engineering skills, based on standards that were the secrets of the builders.

LEFT: Alhambra Cupola: Granada, Spain, c. 1350, Yusuf I, architect. (*Ediciones Sicilia Zaragoza*)
TOP RIGHT: Cathedral Apse: Amiens, France, 1220–1288, Robert de Luzarches, architect. (*Les Éditions d'Art Ivon, Paris*)
BOTTOM RIGHT: De Bijenkorf Department Store: Rotterdam, The Netherlands, 1954, Marcel Breuer, architect. (*Van Ditmar's Press-Import, The Netherlands*)

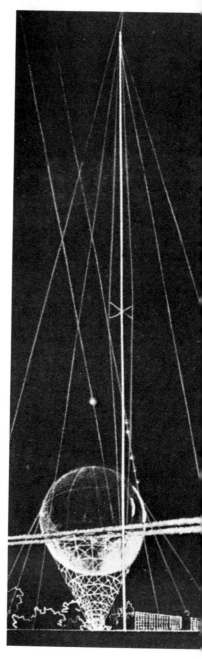

Chiesa di S. Andrea del Quirinale: Rome, Italy, 1670, Giovanni Lorenzo Bernini, architect.

BELOW and RIGHT: Lenin Institute: Moscow, U.S.S.R., c. 1929, J. Leonidow, architect.

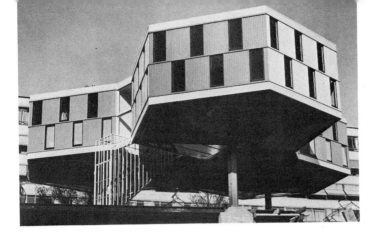

Segments of buildings extended to extreme formal expression

Circular stairs and a circular platform are used as an approach to the circular portico and entrance to S. Andrea del Quirinale; a globe serves as an auditorium for the Lenin Institute; a temporary pavilion for a Rotterdam building site is hexagonal in form, with a running motif along vertical planes that accentuates its free orientation to the space around it; vertically extended dormer windows emphasize the steeply sloping roof of the Château de Josselin. In all these examples, formal elements of the design are clearly, directly stated.

ABOVE: Office for Building Site: Rotterdam, The Netherlands, 1954, Marcel Breuer, architect.
RIGHT: Château de Josselin: Brittany, France, c. 1500.

Stairs as architectural elements on the exteriors of buildings

The functional business of connecting different floors or levels, when it occurs at an exterior wall of a building, presents an opportunity to develop the connecting segment either as a diversified extension of the design of the main mass or as a positive contrast to it. Contrast occurs in the Werkbund Exposition Building, where the glass-enclosed circular stairs are situated at the corner of a solid brick structure. Both on the façade of the Château de Blois and in the corner of the court of the Printer's Union the horizontal spandrels, bent diagonally to follow the stairs, introduce another dimension to the over-all design.

ABOVE LEFT: Château de Blois: Blois, France, 1515–1530. Design of stairs attributed to Leonardo da Vinci. (*Giraudon, Paris*)

RIGHT: Werkbund Exposition Building: Cologne, Germany, 1914, Walter Gropius, architect.

LEFT: Printers' Union: Berlin, Germany, 1930, Max Taut, architect.

ABOVE: Row Housing, Weissenhof: Stuttgart, Germany, 1927, J. J. P. Oud, architect.

LEFT: Haarlem Terrace: Haarlem, The Netherlands, 1612.

BELOW: Neubuhl Housing: Zurich, Switzerland, 1937, Artaria, Haefeli, and others, architects.

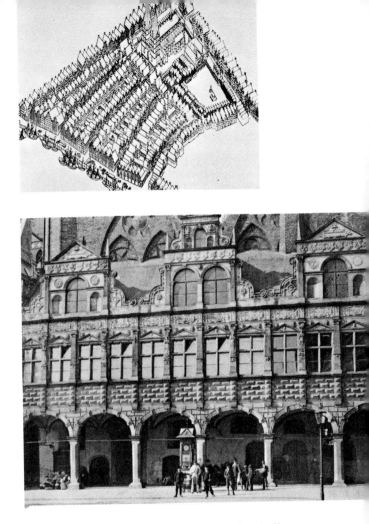

Medieval and Modern row-housing, including a Renaissance city hall, in which repetitive stepped relationships predominate

The commercial centers that grew up in northern Europe during the late Middle Ages and early Renaissance reflected, in their civic atmosphere, the stewardship of an evolving group of self-reliant, skilled, and unpretentious solid citizens—many of them members of building trades groups or of guilds organized for master craftsmen. In accord with their concept of Christian fellowship and brotherhood, none of them was singled out from the others, but each was assured his identity in the general plan of the whole. The same principle was applied to building units. Stepped relationships in design tend to reinforce it by singling out all parts equally.

45

Evolving forms for multicellular habitations

Renaissance palaces built in Italian cities during the 15th and 16th centuries became the prototype for the impersonal multicellular urban habitations that characterized and dominated European—indeed, Western—cities of the 17th, 18th, and 19th centuries. Until the early 20th century these structures were designed to be closely related to the streets and squares they bordered; the result was a pattern of façade architecture.

More recently the apartment house has been conceived as a free-standing entity in the form of a block, slab, or group of slabs frequently arranged in clusters entirely unrelated to the street at the base.

TOP: Czernin Palace: Prague, Czechoslovakia, 17th century, Caratti, Rossi and Maderna, architects. (*ORBIS*)
RIGHT: Society Hill Towers, Model: Philadelphia, Pennsylvania, United States, 1960, I. M. Pei and Associates, architects. (*George Cserna*)
BOTTOM LEFT: Flats, Neustiftgasse: Vienna, Austria, 1911, Otto Wagner, architect.
BOTTOM CENTER: Lake Shore Apartments: Chicago, Illinois, United States, 1951, Ludwig Mies van der Rohe, architect.

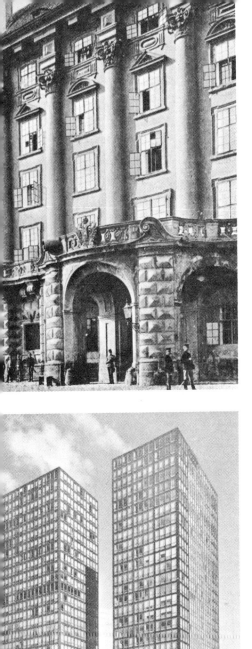

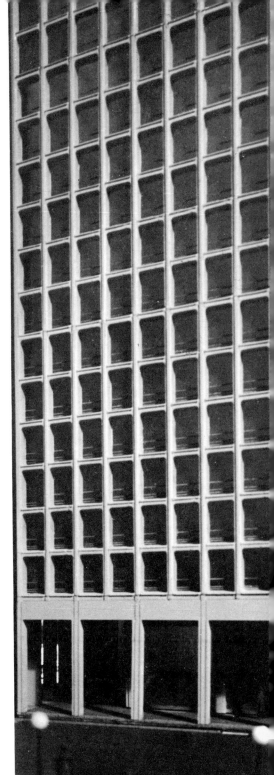

ABOVE: Factory: Kharkov, Ukraine, U.S.S.R., c. 1935, S. S. Serafimoff, M. D. Felguer, S. M. Kravetz, architects.

BELOW: Château d'Usse: Loire region, France, c. 1500. (*R. D'Orange Photos*)

Groupings established by the use of clustered elements

The bridging of blocks and towers of various heights with horizontal elements creates animated architectural groupings that suggest the spirited pageantry of the feudal period, when the architecture harmonized with the quartering occuring in the multicolored costumes and heraldry emblems. In modern art similarly lively juxtapositions are often found. The parallel horizontal connectors in the apartment house shown in the bottom right illustration are planned to serve as community centers, with facilities such as restaurants, lounges, etc.

RIGHT: Basilica and Temple of Poseidon: Paestum, Italy, 450 B.C. (*Brogi Photo*)

BELOW: Air Force Academy: Colorado Springs, Colorado, United States, 1959, Skidmore, Owings, and Merrill, architects. (*Stewarts Commercial Photographers, Inc.*)

BELOW: Palace of Versailles: Versailles, France, 1756, Louis Le Vau, Jules Hardouin-Mansart, Jacques Ange Gabriel, architects. (*X Phot*)

BOTTOM: Treasury of Siphnos, North Frieze: Delphi, Greece, 530–525 B.C.

Groups of buildings architecturally related to planned horizontal surfaces

Buildings with an official purpose are usually surrounded by open areas, which may serve as spaces for processions, pageants, parades, etc. These open areas combine with the buildings to form, with them, an integrated architectural whole. The sculptural friezes, the statuary, and the ordered landscaping reinforce the epic character of the events that take place in these surroundings. The buildings themselves are modulated rhythmically, but in large controlled planar areas that harmonize with the designs of the broad terraces and plazas around them.

RIGHT: Garden and Pond: Vaux-le-Vicomte, France, 1660, André Lenôtre, landscape architect. (*Hélio Catala Frères, Paris*)
FAR RIGHT: Robinson House: Williamstown, Massachusetts, United States, 1946, Marcel Breuer, architect. (*Robert Damora*)

Inclined planes enhance horizontal and vertical relationships

One of the techniques that reach beyond the balanced harmony of buildings and building groups in classic architecture is the introduction of oblique planes into a composition in which the dominant elements are pure cubes, disks, or flat oblong planes in either a vertical or a horizontal position.

CENTER LEFT: Brazil House: Paris, France, 1959, Le Corbusier, architect. (*Lucien Hervé*)
CENTER RIGHT AND FAR RIGHT: Tuberculosis Sanatorium: Paimio, Finland, 1932, Alvar Aalto, architect.
RIGHT: Colonnade, St. Peter's Cathedral: Rome, Italy, 1655–1667, Giovanni Lorenzo Bernini, architect.

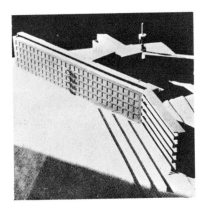

The punctuating effect
of a vertical element
in relation to a horizontal
building mass

The placing of a tower, or
any other vertical element,
against a horizontal compo-
nent of a building block or
group illustrates the effec-
tiveness of balance between
the "dominant" and the
"passive."

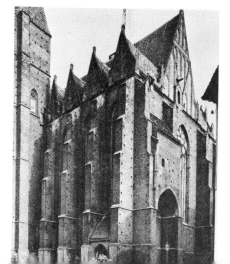

54

TOP LEFT: Tobacco Factory: Rotterdam, The Netherlands, c. 1930, J. A. Brinkman and L. C. van der Vlugt, architects.

TOP RIGHT: I. G. Farben: Höchst am Main, Germany, 1924, Peter Behrens, architect.

RIGHT: Palazzo Saracini, Restoration: Siena, Italy, 14th century. (*Alinari Art Reference Bureau*)

BOTTOM LEFT: Kreuzkirche: Wrocław (Breslau), Poland, c. 1300. (*A. Renger Patzsch*)

BOTTOM RIGHT: Ford Motor Company Steel Mill: Detroit, Michigan, United States, 1917, Albert Kahn, Inc., architects.

Strong horizontal or oblique elements emphasize the nature of essentially vertical structures

The counterpoint of horizontal and vertical building elements can make the principal building form seem more powerful. This idea is clearly illustrated by the design for the Izvestia Building and by the Palazzo Pubblico in Montepulciano. The verticality of the tower in Ulm is reinforced by the diagonal silhouette of the sharply sloping roof.

LEFT: Tower: Ulm, Germany, c. 1300–1400. (*Leonar 79TI*)
RIGHT: Izvestia Building Project: Moscow, U.S.S.R., c. 1930, G. Barchin, architect.
FAR RIGHT, TOP: Palazzo Pubblico: Montepulciano, Italy, c. 1350.
FAR RIGHT, BOTTOM: Palazzo Gotico: Piacenza, Italy, 1281. (*Ed. A. Traldi, Milan*)
BELOW: Hat Factory: Luckenwalde, Germany, 1921, Eric Mendelsohn, architect.

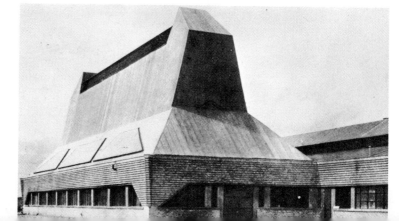

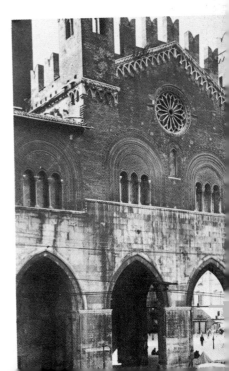

LEFT: Medieval House: Berncastel Cues, Germany, c. 1400. (Cramers Kunstanstalt K.G.)

BELOW: Chapel of Nuestra Señora de la Soledad: San José del Altillo, Coyoacán, Mexico, 1956, Enrique de la Mora y Palomar, architect. (Erwin Lang)

Dramatic effect of a building mass culminating in a pointed roof

The dynamic quality of the culture of the Middle Ages supported the development of the decisively expressive in its building forms.

58

BELOW: Musée Alsacien: Strasbourg, France, c. 1500.

LEFT: First Unitarian Church: Madison, Wisconsin, United States, 1950, Frank Lloyd Wright, architect. (*Ezra Stoller Associates*)

BELOW: Chile-Haus: Hamburg, Germany, 1923, Fritz Hoeger, architect.

ABOVE: S. Maria: Zadar, Yugoslavia, c. 1500.

TOP CENTER: College of San Isidoro: León, Spain, 1067, Master Pedro Vitambén, architect. (*Winocio, León*)

TOP RIGHT: House of Saurau Street: Vienna, Austria, 1913, Adolf Loos, architect.

RIGHT: Maison Jaoul: Neuilly, France, 1958, Le Corbusier, architect. (*Lucien Hervé*)

BELOW: House of the Surveyors of the River, Ideal City: Chaux, France, c. 1800, Claude-Nicolas Ledoux, architect.

Semicircles used as a strong end treatment to a variety of architectural elements

In each of the examples illustrated, the dominant form is the semicircle, emphasized by the casual introduction of oblong openings. These examples have no cultural or functional relationship to one another; they owe their similarity solely to that of their geometric forms.

RIGHT: Fortifications: Naarden, The Netherlands, c. 1650. (*KLM Aerocarto n.v. Airport Amsterdam*)

RIGHT: Iglesia de la Virgen Milagrosa: Mexico City, Mexico, 1955, Felix Candela, engineer, Enrique de la Mora y Palomar, architect. (*Erwin Lang*)

LEFT: Ponte del Paradiso: Venice, Italy, c. 1350. (*Ed. A. Traldi, Milan*)

The apex of a triangle as the dominant factor

Here the triangular motif was chosen in each case for a special reason. In the illustration at the left the apex of the triangle dividing the space between the buildings above accentuates the opening below. In the top right illustration the fortifications have been planned in recognition of the invention and use of firearms in warfare. In the bottom right illustration the structural characteristics of concrete shells determine the forms and arrangement of the building parts.

Impact of twin or multiple apexes in space

The élan of the age of chivalry and medieval religious aspirations toward heaven probably account for the soaring spires that are so characteristic a part of the architecture of the Middle Ages. Similar architectural results are attained today, when the approach to design differs substantially from the formalistic idiom cultivated during the Renaissance; in such modern examples, more emphasis is given to expressive form, arrived at organically, than to balanced harmony. This organic form is closely related to the inner structural system.

LEFT: Church of Tyn Spires, Prague, Czechoslovakia, 14th century. (*Karla Plicky*)

ABOVE: Holstentor: Lübeck, Germany, 1469, Heinrich Helmstede, Stadtbaumeister. (*Wilh. Castelli, Lübeck*)

BELOW: State Fair Arena: Raleigh, North Carolina, United States, 1953, Matthew Nowicki and W. H. Deitrick, architects. (*Chamber of Commerce, Raleigh, North Carolina*)

BELOW: Poème Electronique, International Exhibition: Brussels, Belgium, 1958, Le Corbusier, architect. (*Lucien Hervé*)

ABOVE: Airplane Hangar: Rome, Italy, 1940, Pier Luigi Nervi, architect.

Contrast of solid and void make a vigorous corner treatment

Hollowed-out sculpture has a special quality quite different from the monolithic character of traditional work. In building design the dematerialization of mass was one of the characteristics of Gothic architecture; the porch of St. Urban is a good example of it. In the airplane hangar (*top right*) it happened through structural necessity. In Robie House (*bottom right*) it is a considered effect.

BELOW: Robie House: Chicago, Illinois, United States, 1909, Frank Lloyd Wright, architect. (*Chicago Heritage Committee, photo by R. Nickel*)
LEFT: St. Urban, South Porch: Troyes, France, c. 1270. (*Martin Hürlimann*)

**Clear punctuation by a simple
square or rectangular opening
at the corner of a building**

In otherwise comparatively complex
designs the simple contrast of an area
indicating depth with a flat surface
accentuates the planar qualities of
two walls meeting at a corner.

Gropius House: Dessau, Germany, 1926,
Walter Gropius, architect. (*Lucia Moholy*)

Bradley House: Woods Hole, Massachusetts, United States, 1911, George Grant Elmslie, architect. (*N. Romano*)

Villa Rotunda: Vicenza, Italy, 16th century, Andrea Palladio, architect. (*Alinari Art Reference Bureau*)

The spirit of the age of enlightenment, shown in modest dwellings of the time (c. 1780), still taking effect in some contemporary designs

Characteristic of an attitude prevailing during the age of enlightenment was the demand for a new, more democratic order of society. The rationalism and the questioning skepticism that grew from the scientific methods of men like Descartes and Newton resulted in a deliberate emphasis on sharp simplicity of outline, mass, and surface in building design.

ABOVE: Farmhouse at Cobham: Surrey, England, c. 1750.
RIGHT: Chamberlain Cottage: Wayland, Massachusetts, United States, 1940, Marcel Breuer, Walter Gropius, architects. (Ezra Stoller Associates)

70

LEFT: House at Weissenhof: Stuttgart, Germany, 1927, Walter Gropius, architect. BELOW: Small houses: Tönder, Denmark, c. 1800. (F. Bruckmann K.G., Munich)

RIGHT: Hermann Lange House: Krefeld, Germany, 1928, Ludwig Mies van der Rohe, architect.
BELOW: Harrison Gray Otis House: Boston, Massachusetts, United States, 1807, Charles Bulfinch, architect.
BELOW RIGHT: "Cliveden," Benjamin Chew's House: Philadelphia, Pennsylvania, United States, 1761. (Wayne Andrews)

Accent on dignity in the houses of prominent families from the 18th to the 20th century

From the early 19th century on, the expanding merchant and professional classes tended to accept the formalities developed by the aristocratic culture of the late Renaissance as the appropriate image for residential architecture. However, the spirit of monarchical absolutism was largely rejected and replaced by theories of progress and of the dignity of the individual.

BELOW: Virginia State Capitol: Richmond, Virginia, United States, 1785, Thomas Jefferson and C. L. Clerisseau, architects.

BELOW: Ainsley Hall Residence: Columbia, South Carolina, United States, 1818, Robert Mills, architect. (Wayne Andrews)

Echoes of the Parthenon in various countries about 1800

These are examples of a derived form indiscriminately applied to quite disparate architectural problems. The men of the Neo-Classic period in particular (c. 1800) were inhibited by their increasing knowledge of archaeology and by their associations with it. These associations reflected the beginnings of romanticism, a conscious reaction to the extreme materialism engendered by the then new mechanistic outlook.

LEFT: Parthenon: Athens, Greece, 447–432 B.C., Ictinus, Calicrates, architects. (*V. Marinaros and A. Miracha*)

RIGHT: Villa Foscari: Malcontenta, Italy, 1560, Andrea Palladio, architect.

BELOW: Brandenburg Gate: Berlin, Germany, 1793, Carl Gotthard Langhans, architect.

In 1800 individual dignity was expressed in modest single and repetitive dwelling units

The formality and the emphasis on seemliness honored by a well-established middle class is reflected in the houses of northern Europe and America at the beginning of the industrial expansion that occurred during the 19th century. The design of many modern housing groups reflects a similar recognition of the value of planning for the fulfillment of the basic requirements of the family in a decent and orderly manner.

BELOW: House: Amsterdam, The Netherlands, c. 1800. (F. Bruckmann K.G., Munich)

ABOVE: Row houses: Delft, The Netherlands, c. 1800. (*F. Bruckmann K.G., Munich*)

LEFT: Dolderthal Apartments: Zurich, Switzerland, 1933, Marcel Breuer and A. and E. Roth, architects.

RIGHT: Delancey Place: Philadelphia, Pennsylvania, United States, 1853 (*John R. Wells*)

LEFT: House: St. Albans, England, c. 1800.

Accent on elegance in houses—17th, 18th, and 19th centuries

The subtleties and refinements of the Rococo style and its association with the old aristocratic order remained an influence in residential architecture, both in Europe and in America.

RIGHT: Château de Villarceaux: Île-de-France, France, c. 1650.

BELOW: House: Basel, Switzerland, 1759, Archilles Ryhiner, architect. (*Photoglob-Wehrli AG*)

BELOW: House Muraltengut: Zurich, Switzerland, 1770, Johann Werdmuller, architect. (*Photoglob-Wehrli AG*)

ABOVE: "Westover": Charles City County, Virginia, United States, 1730, William Byrd II, architect. (*Wayne Andrews*)

LEFT: Residence: Lincoln, Massachusetts, United States, 1938, Walter Gropius, architect. (*Editions Girsberger*)

79

Zwingerpavillon: Dresden, Germany, 1722
Matthäus Daniel Poppelmann, architect

Church: Saint-Benoît-sur-Loire, France, 11th century.

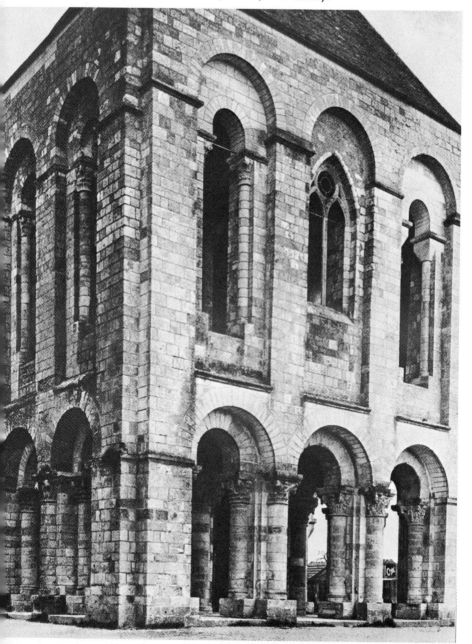

Mosse Pavilion of Pressa:
Cologne, Germany, 1928,
Eric Mendelsohn, architect.

**The appearance of
suspension in space
given by structures
with recessed entrances
in open areas beneath**

The fantastic designs of various periods evoke similar moods, though the architectural forms differ markedly. The Mosse Pavilion, because of its emphasis on the horizontal with barely discernible vertical support, together with its curved, transparent, glistening envelope, seems less earthbound than everyday buildings. In the Rococo Zwingerpavillon Baroque dynamism has been etherealized by a rejection of classical paraphernalia inherited from the Renaissance; as a result, the interlacing of forms and ornaments is free and imaginative.

Spiral, concave, convex, and pierced forms organized in a progression toward a pinnacle

The successful arrangement of multiple elements to build up to a climax is an ever-recurring architectural challenge, which, as illustrated, can be met in a variety of ways.

TOP LEFT: Karlskirche: Vienna, Austria, 1715–1737, Johann Bernhard Fischer von Erlach, architect.

TOP CENTER: S. Andrea della Fratte: Rome, Italy, 17th century, Francesco Borromini, architect.

TOP RIGHT: Monument of the Third International: Moscow, U.S.S.R., 1920, W. Tatlin, architect.

BOTTOM LEFT: S. Satiro: Milan, Italy, 1474, Bramante, architect.

BOTTOM CENTER: Trinity College: Cambridge, England, c. 1600. (*Stearn and Sons, Cambridge*)

BOTTOM RIGHT: Sans Souci: Potsdam, Germany, 1770, George Christian Unger, architect. (*I. Wollstein, Berlin*)

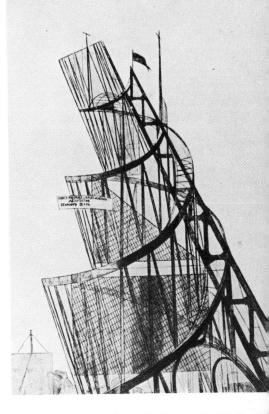

Surface

The surface qualities of a building—texture, pattern, and color—can be used to accentuate or modify the character of external architectural forms and certain kinds of interior space. In addition to enlivening an architectural composition, surface treatment such as the use of ornamental façades, for example, or of an intricate grid as the front of a building, may in itself determine its impact. Pattern can be used to accentuate height, width, or depth; color can be used to modify the quality of light, to make areas recede or be projected, to emphasize a cool or a warm environment, or to create a delicate or complicated balance that will give life to an architectural design. It may be further enriched by the inclusion of transparent, translucent, and reflecting surfaces, as many of the illustrations on the following pages demonstrate.

ABOVE: Casa de los Picos: Segovia, Spain, c. 1550. (*Fototipia de Hauser y Menet, Madrid*)
TOP RIGHT: Stock Exchange, North La Salle Building: Chicago, Illinois, United States, 1893, Dankmar Adler and Louis Sullivan, architects. (*Chicago Heritage Committee, photo by R. Nickel*)
BOTTOM RIGHT: Wohnhauser der "Gehag": Berlin, Germany, c. 1930, Bruno Taut, architect.

**Strong contrast of light and shadow obtained by placement
of window bays, treatment of masonry walls, etc.**

Through the many sharp shadows that are cast when light strikes broken surfaces, vibrant and positive architectural statements can be made. The architectural impact of buildings that use this technique is derived from the technique
itself rather than from the form of the building.

Rusticated walls and piers with arched openings increasing in number at succeeding levels produce an architecture that suggests soundness and massiveness

The imposing effect of large, rugged masonry structures such as Roman aqueducts has been achieved at various periods. Ancient methods have influenced the treatment of the exterior walls of buildings, but the essentially structural character of the earlier models has become less prosaic. The resulting architecture is vigorous. A type of counterpoint between horizontally and vertically developed rhythms follows the changes in treatment at different levels.

TOP LEFT: Aqueduct: Segovia, Spain, c. 200 A.D. (*Fototipia de Hauser y Menet, Madrid*)
TOP RIGHT: Pitti Palace: Florence, Italy, 1440, Filippo Brunelleschi, architect.
BOTTOM LEFT: Cathedral Tower: Zamora, Spain, 1174. (*J. Laurent y Cia, Madrid*)
BOTTOM RIGHT: Marshall Field Wholesale Store: Chicago, Illinois, United States, 1887, H. H. Richardson, architect. (*Chicago Architectural Photographing Co.*)

RIGHT: Fisher Body Company:
Cleveland, Ohio, United States,
c. 1915, Albert Kahn, Inc., architects.
BELOW: Corn Silo, South America,
1910. (*Lucia Moholy*)

ABOVE: Bauhaus: Dessau, Germany, 1926, Walter Gropius,
architect. (*Lucia Moholy*)
LEFT: Royal Crescent: Bath, England, 1775, John Wood the
Younger, architect. (*National
Building Record, London*)

Rhythmical treatment resulting from repetition of identical vertical elements

A simple rhythmical arrangement, whether of multiple silos, engaged columns, structural piers, buttresses, or window mullions on a glass wall, accentuates the diminishing perspective of predominantly horizontal structures.

LEFT: Sandkirche: Wrocław (Breslau), Poland, c. 1200. (A. Renger-Patzsch)
BELOW: A.E.G.: Berlin, Germany, 1912, Peter Behrens, architect.

ABOVE: Guaranty-Prudential Building: Buffalo, New York, United States, 1895, Louis Sullivan, architect. (*Wayne Andrews*)

LEFT: Tower, Isola di Torcello: Venice, Italy (rebuilt), 1008 A.D. (*Stoedner Photo*)

Vertical continuity as a means of emphasizing the character of tall structures

Through definite vertical continuity of treatment, high buildings acquire a soaring quality that could never be achieved through the mere superimposition of elements one upon another. The campanile in Torcello is an early and simple example of such a design, developed through the slightly protruding vertical brick ribs that extend from the base to the summit.

ABOVE: United Nations Building: New York, United States, 1947, Wallace K. Harrison, Le Corbusier, and others, architects. (*Ezra Stoller Associates*)

LEFT: Marienkirche: Stralsund, Germany, c. 1300–1400 (*A. Renger-Patzsch*)

93

The relationship of impersonal building fronts and their horizontally developed repetitive elements to city streets— an important factor in urban architectural character

The sense of never-ending movement along streets is reinforced by an architectural treatment that does not center attention on individual elements but becomes part of an entire metropolitan composition. This treatment is carried to its logical conclusion in the design of the impersonal façades along the Rue de Rivoli in Paris, where no distinction is made between hotels, stores, offices, etc.

ABOVE: Carson, Pirie, Scott Company: Chicago, Illinois, United States, 1904, Louis Sullivan, architect. (*The Art Institute of Chicago*)
BOTTOM LEFT: Rue de Rivoli: Paris, France, c. 1800, Charles Percier and Pierre Fontaine, architects.
BOTTOM CENTER: Berlin Remodeling: Berlin, Germany, 1928, Ludwig Mies van der Rohe, architect.
BOTTOM RIGHT: Grottanelli Palace: Siena, Italy, 13th century.

94

Olivetti Factory: Ivrea, Italy, 1942, Figini and Pollini, architects.

Arena: Nîmes, France, c. 300 A.D. (Lévy et Neurdein Réunis, Paris)

Fluidity achieved by undulating façades

The serpentine movement that results from the curved development of the surfaces of buildings enriches the building groups in a townscape. Subtle shadings and highlights on the rounded planes provide diversity of tone.

LEFT: Pedro Gulho Apartments: Rio de Janeiro, Brazil, 1955, Affonso Eduardo Reidy, architect. (*Aertsens Michel*)

RIGHT: Peterskirche: Vienna, Austria, 1713, Johann Bernhard Fischer von Erlach, architect. (*Reiffenstein, Vienna*)

BELOW: Telschow Building: Berlin, Germany, 1928, Luckhardt Brothers and Alfons Anker, architects.

BELOW RIGHT: Adelaide Crescent: Brighton, England, 1830, Decimus Burton, architect. (*Frederick Gibberd*)

Concave building masses conducive to the play of light and shadow

The plastic development of surfaces and separate members of a building's exterior can approximate a sculptural method of composition in order to arrive at an emphatic design.

ABOVE: Château d'O: Normandy, France, 15th century.
FAR RIGHT: S. Carlo alle Quattro Fontane: Rome, Italy, 1665, Francesco Borromini, architect.
RIGHT: Swiss Pavilion at University City: Paris, France, 1932, Le Corbusier, architect. (*Lucien Hervé*)

Vertical and furrowed units, loosely related, create an unusual spatial effect

The "slipped" relationship of the individual parts to each other gives surfaces, both interior and exterior, a lively movement and, through the relationship of depth to projection, an interesting play of relief.

School of Art, Library: Glasgow, Scotland, 1902, Charles Rennie Mackintosh, architect.

Universalist Church (Unity Church): Oak Park, Illinois, United States, 1906, Frank Lloyd Wright, architect. (Chicago Heritage Committee, photo by R. Nickel)

ABOVE: Castillo Coca: Segovia, Spain, c. 1500. (*J. Laurent y Cia, Madrid*)

BELOW LEFT: Westminster Abbey, Henry VII's Chapel: London, England, 1503–1519, William and Robert Vertue, architects. (*Mansell*)

BELOW RIGHT: Finnish Exhibition, World's Fair: New York, New York, United States, 1939–1940, Alvar Aalto, architect. (*Ezra Stoller Associates*)

The *Art-Nouveau* approach to design was also present in some medieval work

The endlessly swirling linear motifs characteristic of the designs of the *Art-Nouveau* movement imparted a flowing quality as well as an impression of insubstantiality to structures reminiscent of medieval architecture and the appurtenant sculpture. The approach to design in *Art-Nouveau* was determined not only by a naturalistic treatment of romantic subjects but also by a belief that the artisan's contribution to the beauty of our surroundings was of utmost importance—hence the emphasis on exotic detail. The movement was a reaction to conditions attending the industrial revolution and a conscious return to aspects of the medieval period.

Hôtel de Sens: Paris, France, 15th century.

RIGHT: Eiffel Tower: Paris, France, 1889, Alexandre Gustave Eiffel, engineer.

FAR RIGHT: The Solomon R. Guggenheim Museum: New York, New York, United States, 1959, Frank Lloyd Wright, architect.

ABOVE LEFT: Hochzeitsturm: Darmstadt, Germany, 1907, Joseph Olbrich, architect.

ABOVE RIGHT: Park Guell: Barcelona, Spain, c. 1900, Antonio Gaudi, architect. (*Zodiac*)

Compositional value of flat planes with sharply defined rectangular and circular openings, niches, and recesses

The function of the rectangular plane as an element in architectural design becomes more explicit when the plane is perforated by distinctly shaped circles and rectangles. Parallel planes in the form of recesses, or planes in a perpendicular relationship, amplify the design attributes of the original plane.

TOP LEFT AND CENTER: St. James Square Staircase: London, England, 1772, Robert Adam, architect. (*Country Life Ltd.*)
TOP RIGHT: Hayward House: Charleston, South Carolina, United States, 1750.
BOTTOM LEFT: Villa di Papa Giulio III: Rome, Italy, 1550.
BOTTOM RIGHT: Pavillon "L'Esprit Nouveau": Paris, France, 1925, Le Corbusier, architect. (*Lucien Hervé*)

Surfaces made rhythmical through the arrangement of openings, projections, and contrasting materials

Changes in rhythm, whether vertical or horizontal, are important in achieving interesting, animated designs for the external surfaces of buildings. Contrast in adjoining materials heightens realization of the basic architectural concept.

106

TOP LEFT: Flats Rond de Lijnbaan:
Rotterdam, The Netherlands, c.
1950, Bakema and Van den
Broeck, architects. (*Van Ditmar's
Press-Import Holland*)

TOP CENTER: Palazzo Ca' d'Oro:
Venice, Italy, 1430, Giovanni
and Bartolomeo Buon, architects.
(*Cav. P. Fiorentini*)

TOP RIGHT: Unité d'Habitation:
Marseilles, France, 1947–1952,
Le Corbusier, architect. (*Lucien
Hervé*)

BOTTOM LEFT: Queen's College:
Cambridge, England, c. 1700.
(*Stearn and Sons, Cambridge*)

BOTTOM RIGHT: House: Lake of
Geneva, Switzerland, 1904,
Adolf Loos, architect.

ABOVE: Spiesshof: Basel, Switzerland, 1500–1600. (*Photoglob-Wehrli AG*)

ABOVE RIGHT: Maison du Peuple: Como, Italy, 1936, Giuseppe Terragni, architect.

RIGHT: Millowners' Association Building: Ahmadabad, India, 1954, Le Corbusier, architect. (*Lucien Hervé*)

FAR RIGHT: S. Maria della Pace: Rome, Italy, 1500, Bramante, architect. (*Alinari Art Reference Bureau*)

Open grid applied to vertical surfaces permits both ample entry and control of light

In conditions where dazzling sunlight taxes the limits of human comfort an open grid can be designed to admit daylight yet provide the needed shade. In northern climates, where the sunlight is less intense, the open grid is designed merely to admit the greatest possible amount of daylight. In each case the grid becomes an important element architecturally.

Sharp contrasts in light and dark make incisive patterns on the exterior surfaces of buildings

ABOVE: Fleischalle: Haarlem, Holland, 1603, Lievan de Key, architect.

Vivid patterns evolving from an arrangement of contrasting materials or of solids and voids exemplify the importance of the master craftsman's contribution to certain phases of architectural development—an importance due to the competent artist's or designer's special understanding of the particular nature and quality of each material used and his innate self-assurance in the manipulation of it.

110

ABOVE: United States Embassy: The Hague, The Netherlands, Marcel Breuer, architect. (*Jan Vershel*)

RIGHT: Little Moreton Hall: Cheshire, England, c. 1500.
BELOW: S. Giovanni Fuorcivitas: Pistoia, Italy, 12th century. (*Alinari Art Reference Bureau*)

S. Maria la Nuova: Monreale, Sicily, Italy, 12th century.

Stoclet Palace: Brussels, Belgium, 1910,
Josef Hoffman, architect. (*Max Taut*)

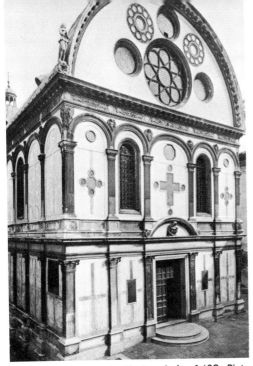

S. Maria dei Miracoli: Venice, Italy, 1489, Pietro Lombardo, architect. (*Alinari Art Reference Bureau*)

Soane's House: London, England, c. 1800, John Soane, architect.

Flat and curved surfaces accentuated through the use of decorative outlines (along edges)

The outlining and subdividing of surfaces with borders of a contrasting material which are also molded and enriched in detail is an established way of emphasizing the special beauty of flat marble panels or of other flush materials used as facings for exterior walls of buildings.

113

TOP LEFT AND CENTER: Propylaea: Athens, Greece, 432 B.C., Mnesicles, architect. (*A. Genthe; Plischke and Muschenheim*)
TOP RIGHT: Porta Aurea in Diocletian's Palace: Split, Yugoslavia, 300 A.D.
BOTTOM LEFT: Court of Justice: Chandigarh, India, 1960, Le Corbusier, architect. (*Valerie Winter*)
BOTTOM RIGHT: Thannhauser Art Gallery: Berlin; Germany, c. 1930, Luckhardt and Anker, architects.

The entrance as an architecturally emphatic preparation for the specific interior

In four different architectural vernaculars—Greek, Roman, Modern 1930, and Modern 1960—basic, purely architectural elements have been organized to accentuate the transition from external to internal space. The distinctive characteristics of the architectural elements illustrated are the contrasting sizes of openings, the use of reveals and recesses as foils for the play of light and shadow, and surface treatments capable of bringing out special qualities of the material, whether stone, glass or concrete.

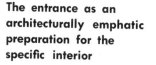

114

Extravagant screens serving as fronts for buildings

Attention to the development of decorative detail is illustrated in these medieval, Baroque, *Art-Nouveau*, and contemporary façades of a predominately ornamented nature. The effect of depth given by the random openings is increased by the continuity of light and shadow that results from the plastic treatment of surfaces.

TOP LEFT: McGregor Memorial Conference Center: Detroit, Michigan, United States, 1958, Minoru Yamasaki, architect. (*Balthazar Korab*)

TOP RIGHT: Department Store: Berlin, Germany, 1904, Alfred Messel, architect.

BOTTOM LEFT: Cathedral: Murcia, Spain, 1700–1750 James Bort, architect.

BOTTOM RIGHT: Wells Cathedral: Wells, England, early 13th to 15th centuries. (*Mansell*)

LEFT: Cathedral: Rouen, France, 12th–15th centuries. (*Photo CAP/© SPADEM 1964 by French Reproduction Rights, Inc.*)

BELOW: Alhambra: Granada, Spain, c. 1350, Yusuf I, Muhammad V, architects. (*Senan y Gonzales*)

An effect of mystery achieved through perforated or transparent surfaces in Arabic, medieval, and modern examples

The quality characterizing the design of medieval cathedrals sometimes appears in other types of building. Covering the outside of a building with transparencies or ornamental modulations of the surface creates a kind of veil that makes what is behind it seem mysterious.

118

Court Building: Chandigarh, India, 1957, Le Corbusier, architect. (*Ernst Sheidegger, Zurich*)

Cathedral: Strasbourg, France, c. 1300–1350, Johannes and Gerlach Erwin, architects.

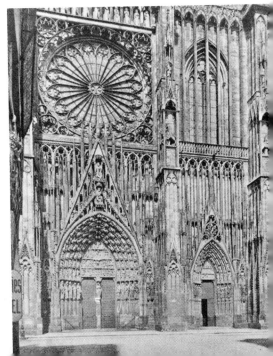

Sculpture and surface treatment at a high artistic level blend with architecture

Architects have collaborated for generations with painters, sculptors, and artisans. The contributions of artists to the significance of architecture are extremely important. When, for spatial or other reasons, a patterned surface or a sculptural element is required, continuity and depth in relation to the total design are possible only when the architect works closely with an artist of stature.

ABOVE: Book-Printers' Union: Berlin, Germany, 1930, Max Taut, architect, relief by Rudolf Belling.

CENTER LEFT: Goldnes Dachl, Fürstenburg Palace: Innsbruck, Austria, c. 1500.
CENTER RIGHT: Pulpit, Cathedral: Torcello, Italy (rebuilt), 1008 A.D.
TOP RIGHT: Balcony of Casa de las Conchas: Salamanca, Spain, 1483. (*Libreria A. Garcia*)

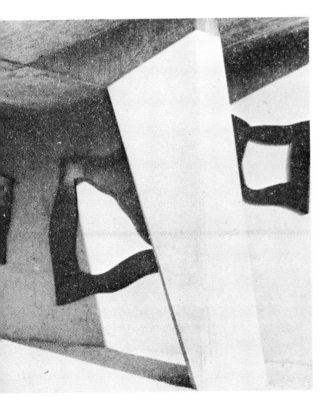

FAR LEFT: Harvard University, Graduate Center: Cambridge, Massachusetts, United States, 1949, Walter Gropius, architect; wall mosaic by Herbert Bayer. (*Robert Damora*)
LEFT: Unesco Building, Sculpture: Paris, France, 1958, Jean Arp, Marcel Breuer, architects. ("*L'Architecture d'aujourd'hui,*" Boulogne, France)

Space

The problems of proportion, scale, rhythm, harmony, and contrast are related to space as well as to form. Other, more specific architectural considerations relating to space are enclosure, height, width, depth, light, and extension. The simple containment of space by walls, floors, and ceiling becomes an interesting and complex problem when subdivision and articulation are required; also when such relationships as those of one space to another, of interior to exterior, of one level to another, and of horizontal to vertical are elaborated. Through the centuries, architects have utilized relationships of space to create extraordinary and emphatic compositions of widely differing character and mood.

Contained exterior spaces obtained by juxtaposition of building masses

Medieval courtyards and open squares are notable for the dynamically balanced relationships achieved by asymmetrical groupings of such dissimilar elements as window bays, turrets, staircases, and large building masses with steeply sloping roofs.

During the Renaissance and to a great extent during the Baroque period that followed it, a more unified spatial scheme was the ideal. In Baroque courtyards and squares, however, the dominant mass was often complex in form. Modern building groups synthesize—at times effectively—the asymmetry of medieval examples and the over-all unity stressed in Renaissance work.

TOP: Bauhaus: Dessau, Germany, 1926, Walter Gropius, architect. (*Lucia Moholy*)

BOTTOM LEFT: Palace of Justice: Rouen, France, c. 1500. (Photo CAP/©SPADEM, 1964 by French Reproduction Rights, Inc.)

BOTTOM RIGHT: National (Royal) Library: Vienna, Austria, 1722, Johann Bernhard Fischer von Erlach, architect.

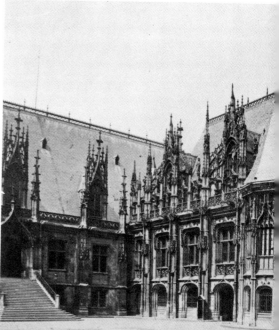

Columns and steps connecting diverse levels in public buildings

In buildings that house objects of special interest, such as the treasures in a museum or the sanctuary in a religious structure, these objects may become focal points. The progression toward them is often developed architecturally through a succession of platforms and steps separated by clusters of columns and spur walls. The groupings are arranged to emphasize spatially the transition from an outer world to an inner world. To a lesser extent, this kind of architectural execution is to be found in some of the more elaborate residential work.

TOP LEFT: Propylaea: Athens, Greece, 432 B.C., Mnesicles, architect. (*Alinari Art Reference Bureau*)

TOP RIGHT: Statue of a Kneeling Woman: Olympia, Greece, c. 460 B.C. (*Marburg-Art Reference Bureau*)

BOTTOM LEFT: Stoclet Palace: Brussels, Belgium, 1910, Josef Hoffman, architect.

BOTTOM CENTER AND RIGHT: Altes Museum, Berlin, Germany, c. 1825, Karl Friedrich Schinkel, architect.

127

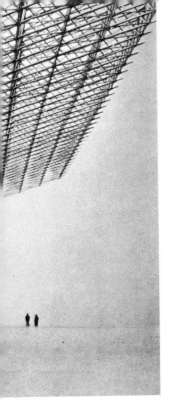

TOP LEFT: Space Frame for an Airplane Hangar: Experimental Project, 1958, Konrad Wachsmann, architect.
TOP RIGHT: Bandshell, Instituto Mexicano del Siguro Social: Santa Fe, Mexico, 1957, Mario Pani, architect, Felix Candela, engineer. (*Erwin Lang*)
BOTTOM LEFT: Fountain: Istanbul, Turkey, c. 1550.
BOTTOM RIGHT: Bandshell, Normal School of Guadalajara: Guadalajara, Mexico, 1957, engineer Felix Candela, architect. (*Erwin Lang*)

Inclined overhang relates protected areas to broad open areas

The unique scale of the overhang on the kiosk pavilion (*bottom left*), which broadly embraces the wide spaces around the fountain, suggests a situation that can be solved even more felicitously with modern structural methods. Islamic culture is based on scientific knowledge and a search for truth exemplified in Islamic architecture by a functional approach to architectural problems, however poetically consummated. This emphasis on a scientific outlook is related to the approach professed by many architects of our time.

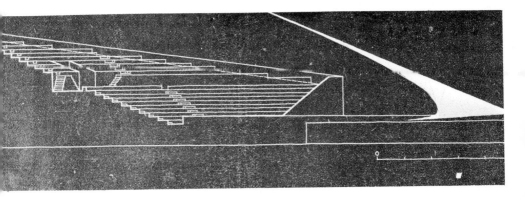

TOP LEFT: Bridge: Lancy, Switzerland, 1936–54, Robert Maillart, engineer. (*Editions Girsberger*)

TOP RIGHT: Exposition Hall: Turin, Italy, 1950, Pier Luigi Nervi, architect.

BOTTOM LEFT: Galerie des Machines: #157 International Exhibition, Paris, 1889 (destroyed 1910), Contamin, engineer. (From *L'Exposition Universelle de 1867 Illustrée*.)

BOTTOM RIGHT: Palacio de la Audiencia: Barcelona, Spain, c. 1400. (*MAS*)

Spatial result of the contrast of broad, arched structures with small, vertical elements

The tension between opposites in a design confirms the particular qualities of each. The opposition of great strength and tenuous delicacy is illustrated in the courtyard of the Palacio de la Audiencia in Barcelona, where the staircase, supported by a wide masonry arch, is backed by a gallery with extremely slender stone columns. Similarly, but perhaps less intentionally, the effect of the great steel arches in the Galerie des Machines is amplified by the narrow vertical mullions of the glass walls.

Airplane Hangar: Rome, Italy, 1950, Pier Luigi Nervi, architect.

Stadtkirche: Freudenstadt, Germany, c. 1500.

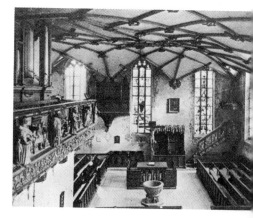

Spatial quality resulting from contrast between vaulted diagrid and flat perpendicular surfaces

The distinct character of the ceilings, resulting from a precise reflection of the structural systems employed, is enhanced by the no less uncompromising treatment of the flat supporting or fill-in walls, which act as a complement in the total design.

Parlatorium in Monastery: Maulbronn, Germany, c. 1450. (*Werkstatte K. Henseling, Maulbronn*)

Sharp, positive contrast of surface forms and materials

The function of the flush plane surface, whether stucco, marble, or mosaic, as an element in design is pointed up when it is juxtaposed with a contrasting element such as a vaulted and/or decorated ceiling, a projecting plane, perforations such as window openings, or a supporting colonnade.

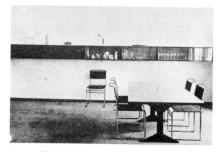

ABOVE: Piscator Apartment: Berlin, Germany, 1929, Marcel Breuer, architect.

LEFT: Santa Sophia: Istanbul, Turkey, 532–537 A.D., Anthemius of Tralles and Isidorus of Miletus, architects. (*Librairie Tchiftdji*)

TOP CENTER: Municipal Library: Viipuri, Finland, 1927–1935, Alvar Aalto, architect. (*Photograph, courtesy The Museum of Modern Art, New York. Photo: Morton Shand*)

TOP RIGHT: S. Apollinare Nuovo: Ravenna, Italy, 6th century.

BOTTOM RIGHT: Palazzo dell' Arte della Seta: Florence, Italy, 16th century. (*Alinari Art Reference Bureau*)

135

Interior and exterior composition of translucent walls in medieval and modern churches

The spatial quality peculiar to medieval church interiors results from the designers' efforts to give an illusion of endless space and to find a source of light conducive to worship. This effort led to the creation of vast translucent surfaces composed of multi-colored glass inserts in a framework of intricate stone tracery. In modern work the problem of furnishing filtered light is handled in a similar way, but a concrete grid or steel framework is substituted for the stone tracery.

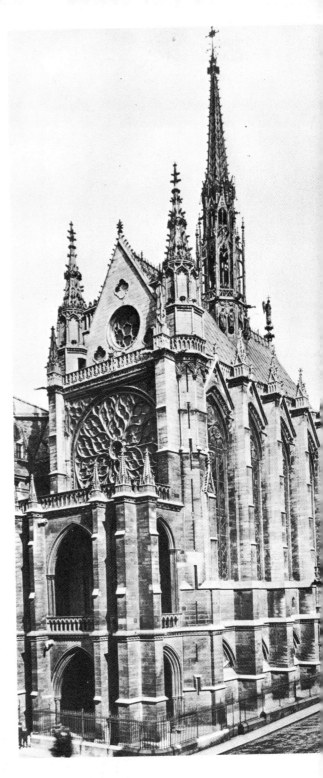

TOP: Notre Dame de Raincy: Le Raincy, France, c. 1925. Auguste Perret, architect.

RIGHT AND CENTER TOP: Sainte Chapelle: Paris, France, 1248, Pierre de Montreuil, architect. (X Photo)

BOTTOM LEFT: Evangelical Church "Pressa": Cologne, Germany, 1928, Otto Bartning, architect.

BOTTOM CENTER: Chartres Cathedral: Chartres, France, 13th century. (Cliché Houvet)

Use of pattern as an important element in the organization of interior spaces

Spatial emphasis can be given to height, breadth, depth, etc., through a knowing, deliberate application of appropriate patterns on walls and ceiling.

TOP LEFT: Liechtenstein Schloss: Feldsberg, Czechoslovakia, 18th century.
TOP CENTER: Marx Residence: Hinter Brühl, Austria, 1911, Josef Hoffman, architect. (*Max Taut*)
TOP RIGHT: Schloss Haanberg bei Brixen: Tirol, Austria, 1510.
BOTTOM LEFT: Syon House, Drawing Room: Middlesex, England, 1762, Robert Adam, architect. (*Country Life Ltd.*)
BOTTOM RIGHT: Interior, Gropius House: Dessau, Germany, 1926, Walter Gropius, architect.

Weblike domed structures provide gossamer envelope for interior space

The master craftsmen and builders of the Gothic period in Europe chose linear and polygonal treatment as appropriate for expressing the religious function of building elements; at the same time, they fitted those into a graphic geometric modular system. In modern work comparable results are obtained through a scientific approach to structural problems.

TOP LEFT: Cathedral, Capilla del Condestable: Burgos, Spain, 1482, Hans of Cologne, architect. (*Fototipia de Hauser y Menet, Madrid*)

TOP CENTER: Ceiling, School in Berkshire: Berkshire, England, c. 1950, Bridgewater and Shepheard, architects, Felix J. Samuely, engineer.

TOP RIGHT: Minster Cathedral, Interior of Tower: Freiburg, Germany, c. 1300.

FAR LEFT: Geodesic Dome: United States, c. 1950, Buckminster Fuller, architect.
LEFT: Lamella Roof, Eugene Sports Arena: Oregon, United States, c. 1950, Lawrence and Holford, architects. (*Timber Structures Inc., Portland, Oregon*)

141

**Modern, engineered slabs
with ribs are similar
spatially to late
medieval ribbed
and vaulted structures**

After the High Gothic period, with its formally systematized ribbed vaults in which the ribs sprang from piers and capitals, a freer spatial result was sought. The new style, a decorative interlacing of ribs growing out of slender columns and merging with walls, is illustrated in the hall-type churches and other buildings of the late 15th century. It is a reflection of the mood of the reformation—a more worldly outlook mingled with a residue of mystical introspection.

The unified interior space encompassed by the undulating flow of the ribs is again achieved in modern work, where the approach to the design of the ribs is not prescribed by decorative intent.

BELOW: Vladislav Hall in the Castel: Prague, Czechoslovakia, c. 1500. (*Karla Plicky*)

142

Kapitelsaal, Monastery: Maulbronn, Germany, c. 1300. (*Werkstatte K. Henseling, Maulbronn*)

The Lonha, Exchange: Palma, Spain, 1426, Guillermo Sagrera, architect. (*G.I.F.A.G.*)

ABOVE: Gatti Wool Factory: Rome, Italy, 1953, Pier Luigi Nervi, architect.

Interior spaces designed especially for festive events

Weikersheim Palace: Württemberg, Germany, 1605.

To provide the appropriate setting for joyous occasions, an informal, animated spatial arrangement is needed. This design concept may be realized in many ways. In the great hall of the Weikersheim Palace, white plaster walls, on which protruding antlers are surrounded by loosely related decorative frescoes, contrast brightly with ceiling paintings framed in a wood grid. In the Redoutensaal in Vienna, the free disposition of platforms, balconies, hanging chandeliers, and stucco decorations merging walls with ceiling fittingly accommodates the bustle of a masked ball. In the University Hall in the Netherlands contrasting, unattached planes of color are organized in a bold and spirited manner.

144

University Hall Project: The Netherlands, 1923,
Theo van Doesburg, C. van Eesteren, architects.

City in Space, Exhibit: Paris,
France, 1925, Frederick Kiesler,
architect.

Redoutensaal: Vienna, Austria,
18th century.

Palazzo Ca' d'Oro, Galleria Franchetti: Venice, Italy, 1430, Giovanni and Bartolomeo Buon, architects. (Cav. P. Fiorentini)

Concert-Hall Project, 1942, Ludwig Mies van der Rohe, architect.

Containment of space through free handling of planar elements

The spatial treatment of St. Stephen's, Walbrook, designed by Sir Christopher Wren at the end of the 17th century, differs, in its emphasis on planar relationships that approach direct expression of the church's wood structure, from the plastic treatment prevailing in Continental Baroque of the period. In earlier buildings—for example, in the Ca' d'Oro in Venice—the separation of planes in space had been the most noticeable characteristic. This concept is carried to its ultimate fulfillment in Mies van der Rohe's concert-hall project (*left center*), but it is embodied even in the central staircase hall of the palace in Bruchsal, an important example of late Continental Baroque architecture. The plane of the circular platform, surrounded by the staircase emanating from below, is singularly effective because it seems to hover freely in space.

LEFT: Episcopal Palace, Central Staircase: Bruchsal, Germany, 1732, Balthasar Neumann, architect.
RIGHT: St. Stephen's, Walbrook: London, England, 1679, Sir Christopher Wren, architect.

Interior spatial development through use of flat curved surfaces

The warped or curved plane, whether it is part of the wall or ceiling or a detached element, is extraordinarily successful in effecting a gentle sense of enclosure. The quality of each plane may be confirmed by appropriate surface treatment, such as thin slabs of marble or wood veneer, which provides evidence of its flatness; by perforation similar to the oval oeils-de-boeuf in the vault of the hall in Schloss Frain; or by an emphasis of the contour, like that which gives the interior of the Pazzi chapel in Santa Croce in Florence its special quality.

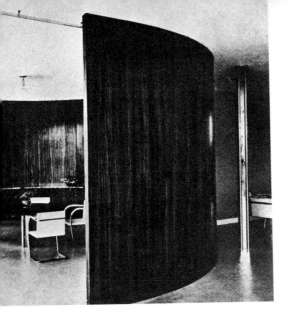

TOP LEFT: Pazzi Chapel, Santa Croce: Florence, Italy, 1430, Filippo Brunelleschi, architect. (*Alinari Art Reference Bureau*)

TOP RIGHT: Tugendhat House: Brno, Czechoslovakia, 1930, Ludwig Mies van der Rohe, architect.

BOTTOM LEFT: Schloss Frain: Frain, Austria, c. 1700, Johann Bernhard Fischer von Erlach, architect.

BOTTOM RIGHT: Santa Sophia: Istanbul, Turkey, 532–537 A.D., Anthemius of Tralles and Isidorus of Miletus, architects. (*Dogan Kardes*)

Graceful fluidity due to continuity of wall and ceiling treatment

When the multiple shafts of Gothic columns merge with the intersecting ribs of the vaulting in the church in Dinkelsbühl, Germany, an exceptionally homogeneous spatial effect is achieved; it has a noticeable flowing quality quite distinct from the static homogeneity of classical architecture. Similar effects may be observed in two later buildings. In the Rococo interior of the Prince Bishop's Palace in Kremsier, Czechoslovakia, both walls and ceilings use a subtly undulating linear treatment, and in the Post Office Savings Bank in Vienna, designed by Otto Wagner, the metal framework for the translucent panels unites with the steel columns and the floor pattern.

Prince Bishop's Palace: Kroměříž (Kremsier), Czechoslovakia, 17th century.

LEFT: St. George's Church: Dinkelsbühl, Germany, 1444–1499. (*Verlag A. Hermann and Co., Stuttgart, Germany.*) RIGHT: Post Office Savings Bank, Vienna, Austria, 1905, Otto Wagner, architect.

Elements dissociated from the basic volume of interior space contribute to spatial vitality

Complexity in the spatial quality of interiors appears in late Gothic, Baroque, and some modern architecture. The Gothic search for a spiritually unifying, all-encompassing architectural space tended to develop forms of expression outside, and more profound than, the classical concepts of balance and self-sufficiency. The Baroque approach to design emphasizes movement, which leads to what Sigfried Giedion has called the "perception of infinity through a dynamic complexity of space."

Auditorium, University of Caracas: Caracas, Venezuela, 1956, Villenueva, architect; clouds designed by sculptor Alexander Calder. (*Life Magazine and Lisa Larsen © 1956 Time Inc. All rights reserved.*)

LEFT: Lorenzkirche: Nürnberg, Germany, 1445–1472, Konrad Roritzer, architect. (*Deutscher Kunstverlag, München-Berlin*)
RIGHT: Kaisersaal: Würzburg, Germany, 1750, Balthasar Neumann, architect.

M.I.T. Dormitory: Cambridge, Massachusetts, United States, 1948, Alvar Aalto, architect. (*Ezra Stoller Associates*)

Exceptional spatial effects obtained by the juxtaposition of oblique forms and planes

Hans Scharoun's design for Philharmonia Hall in Berlin reveals an impressively complex interior spatial concept. The complete rejection of traditional opera-house formality and glitter is attained by a purposeful scrambling of seating groups, wall planes, and floating acoustic panels generally trapezoidal or otherwise irregular in shape. A similar principal of design can be recognized in the Massachusetts Institute of Technology dormitory building designed by Alvar Aalto, as well as in the medieval streets, building groups, and vaulting shown in the other three illustrations.

Philharmonia Project: Berlin, Germany, 1957, Hans Scharoun, architect.

FAR LEFT: Street Scene, Tower of the Cenciaioli Palace: Bologna, Italy, 1400–1500. (*G. Vettori, Bologna*)

LEFT: Sandkirche, Vaulting: Wrocław (Breslau), Poland, c. 1375. (*A. Renger-Patzsch*)

RIGHT: Basilica S. Francesco: Assisi, Italy, c. 1300. (*Ed. Assunti, Assisi*)

Religious buildings showing abstraction in spatial arrangements, art forms, and use of light

Emphasis on the mystical characterizes the architecture of the Byzantine period, when Christianity was becoming the outstanding influence in the Western world. Nevertheless, in church architecture nothing was excluded; every existing thing was represented in its place, from objects of the lowest to those of the highest order. A broad scope of artistic creativity was encouraged in every detail; the resulting work was exempt from formal rules but expressed an intense desire on the part of the builders and architects to represent the Christian religion through the use of appropriate artistic symbols and architectural forms.

In some of the important architectural work of our own time, abstract rather than matter-of-fact or formal interior spaces have been conceived. This modern conception is the result of an attitude which possibly first took form during the Early Christian and Byzantine periods.

TOP LEFT: Church: Vuoksenniska, Finland, 1958, Alvar Aalto, architect. (Jane Davis Doggett/ Dorothy C. Jackson, Architectural Graphics Association, Inc.)

BOTTOM LEFT: S. Vitale: Ravenna, Italy, 547 A.D. (Alinari Art Reference Bureau)

ABOVE: S. Apollinare Nuovo: Ravenna, Italy, 6th century.

BELOW LEFT: Ronchamp Chapel: Ronchamp, France, 1955, Le Corbusier, architect. (Paul Balthasar)

BELOW CENTER AND RIGHT: Guell Colony Chapel: Barcelona, Spain, 1898–1930, Antonio Gaudi, architect. (Juan Prats)

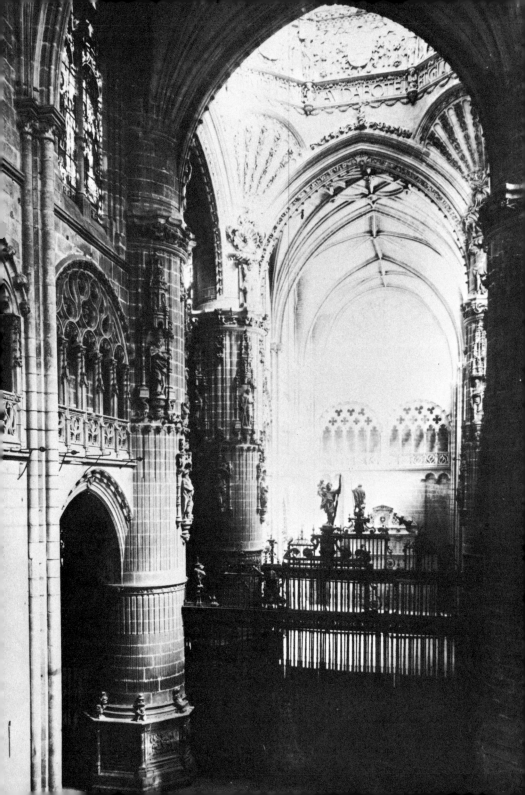

Centralized light from above stressing architectural and spatial concepts

The predominantly sculptural quality of the interiors illustrated is emphasized by the admission of overhead light strategically located in the center, where a climactic spatial culmination occurs. The highlights, shadows, and shadings caused by the downward flow of light disclose the molded forms and chiseled surfaces.

TOP RIGHT: National (Royal) Library: Vienna, Austria, c. 1750, Johann Bernhard Fischer von Erlach, architect.

BOTTOM RIGHT: I. G. Farben: Höchst am Main, Germany, Peter Behrens, architect.

LEFT: Cathedral: Burgos, Spain, 1221–1457, Hans of Cologne and others, architects. (*J. Laurent y Cia, Madrid*)

Spatial effects of domination
by ceiling painting, vaulting, etc.

A vaulted ceiling is normally the larg-
est independent surface in an interior
space, and its treatment will be the
strongest factor determining the spatial character of a room. In the large
gallery of the Schönbrunn Palace in
Vienna the ceiling paintings, elegantly
framed in casual ovaloid forms with
two hanging chandeliers spaced between the three ovals, lend an easy
grace to an otherwise fairly traditional treatment of an oblong hall.
In the Yale skating rink by Eero
Saarinen a central girder divides the
suspended vaults; the girder and
vaults, together, create an unusually
interesting interior space. The main
hall in the Lüneburg Rathaus, whose
walls are composed of diversely
shaped windows, doors, fireplace,
etc., is contained spatially by the simple, segmented arch vault; the entire
surface of the vault is decorated with
the motifs appearing in segmented
forms on the walls. In the chapter
room of the new cathedral in Salamanca the difference in scale between
the lierne ribbed vaults and the framed
niches, doors, and panels underneath
the horizontal band dividing the two
is what gives the space its peculiarly
vague and richly composite character.

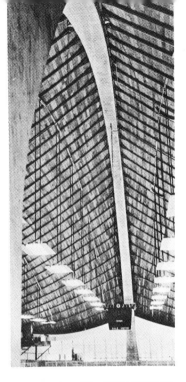

ABOVE: Rathaus, Main Hall: Lüneburg,
Germany, c. 1400–1500.
LEFT: Yale Skating Rink: New Haven,
Connecticut, 1960, Eero Saarinen, arch-
itect. (*Architectural Beacon*)

ABOVE: New Cathedral, Chapter Room: Salamanca, Spain, c.
1500, Juan Gilde Ontañón, architect. (*J. Laurent y Cia, Madrid*)
LEFT: Schönbrunn Palace: Vienna, Austria, 1696,
Johann Bernhard Fischer von Erlach, architect.

Cathedral: Seville, Spain, 1402–1520, Isambret, Carlin, Rodriquez, and others, architects.

Composite interior space achieved through emphasis on vaulting

A composite character is developed in interiors when the supporting elements for the vaults are not part of the walls but occur as separate columns, compound columns, or piers standing freely and unattached in a general enclosure. The manifold subdivisions obtained in this kind of plan result in a complex spatial totality.

LEFT: Factory: Coyoacán, Mexico, 1959, Felix Candela, architect. RIGHT: Sultan Ahmed I, Blue Mosque: Istanbul, Turkey, 1609–1616, Mehmet Aga, architect. (*Librairie Tchiftdji*)

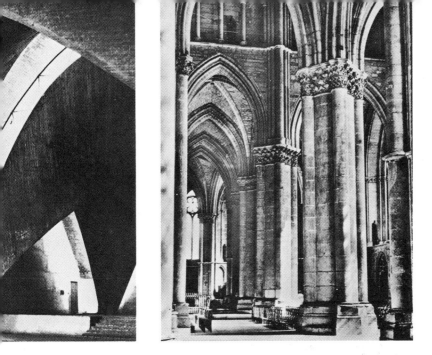

ABOVE LEFT: San Antonio de las Huertas: Mexico City, Mexico, 1959, Felix Candela, architect. (*Jane Davis Doggett/Dorothy C. Jackson, Architectural Graphics Association, Inc.*)

ABOVE RIGHT: Notre Dame Cathedral: Reims, France, 13th century. (*Service Commercial Monuments Historiques*)

The subdivision of space by columns
architecturally related to interior areas

Another type of space results when the columns, rather than the supported vaults or overhead structure, dominate an interior and, though they act as subdividers, stand out as separate sculptural entities in an otherwise largely unified area.

TOP LEFT: Convento dos Jeronymos: Lisbon, Portugal, 1500–1600, Boutica and João de Castilho, architects. (*Kidder Smith*)
CENTER: Exhibition Building (The Palace of Labor): Turin, Italy, 1961, Pier Luigi Nervi, architect-engineer. (*Instituto Italiano di Cultura*)
TOP RIGHT: Maulbronn Monastery: Maulbronn, Germany, 1230. (*Werkstatte K. Henseling, Maulbronn*)
BOTTOM RIGHT: Strasbourg Cathedral, South Transept: Strasbourg, France, 12th–13th centuries.

TOP LEFT: The Château: Chambord, France, 1519–1535, Pierre Nepveu, architect. (*A. Papeghin, Paris, Tours*)

ABOVE: Double Stair: Graz, Austria, 1400–1500.

LEFT: Metal Workers' Union: Berlin, Germany, 1929, Eric Mendelsohn, architect.

RIGHT: Barberini Palace: Rome, Italy, 1638, Giovanni Lorenzo Bernini, architect.

Sculptural attributes of spiral staircases

The convoluted form of a circling stairway, seen either from within or from without, possesses the multi-faceted quality of a complex sculptural composition.

Staircases contribute to the spatial development of interiors

Whether a staircase is designed so elaborately that it suggests—as do the golden staircase in the cathedral at Burgos and the main staircase at Schloss Brühl by the famous Baroque master, Balthasar Neumann—the descent of a waterfall from one level to another, or whether it is designed as a simple, oblique element with a box-like landing and flat, screened guardrail (*top center and bottom left*), it not only fulfills a perfectly evident functional assignment, but also becomes a prominent instrument in generating a dramatic sense of succession from one area to another. In the Restaurant Gurmenia and the Olivetti showroom, the staircases establish an architectural relationship between the balconies and the main space.

Restaurant Gurmania: Berlin, 1928, L. Nachtlicht, architect.

BELOW LEFT: Palazzo Ca' d'Oro, Galleria Franchetti: Venice, Italy, 1421–1436, Giovanni and Bartolomeo Buon, architects. (*Cav. P. Fiorentini*)
BELOW: Cathedral, Staircase: Burgos, Spain, 1519, Diego de Siloé, builder. (*MAS, Barcelona*)

Olivetti Showroom: New York, New York, United States, 1955, Belgioioso, Peressutti, and Rogers, architects. ("L'Architecture d'aujourd'hui," Boulogne, France)

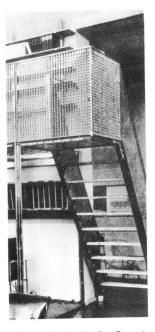

Library Stairs, Berlin Exposition: Berlin, Germany, 1931, Walter Gropius, architect. (*Editions Albert Morancé, Paris*)
RIGHT: Schloss Brühl: Brühl, Germany, c. 1700, Balthasar Neumann, architect.

Forest of columns with arched or vaulted bracing gives a strong sense of perspective

The regular repetition of identical units receding in space develops a considerable sense of depth, which is the essential spatial quality of the interiors illustrated. The system of such a scheme can be readily understood by an inspection of the plan of the mosque at Córdoba (*top right*).

TOP: Mosque (and floor plan): Córdoba, Spain, 786–990 A.D. BOTTOM LEFT: Competition for the Railway Terminus: Naples, Italy, 1956, Project of Castiglioni, Sianesi, Bongioanni. (*"L'Architecture d'aujourd'hui,"* Boulogne, France) BOTTOM RIGHT: Johnson Wax Company Office Building: Racine, Wisconsin, 1939, Frank Lloyd Wright, architect. (*Reinhold Publishing* Co.)

171

Structural systems developing illusions of endless space

The interiors of the great Gothic cathedrals of Europe are significant because they were designed to express in space the theory that the absolute is a spiritually unifying principle without finite bounds. The theory led to an extension of the members of the structural system into continuous linear patterns intersecting in pointed arches. The effect of endlessness basic to the underlying concept was augmented by the towering height. The Baroque park (*bottom center*) was also consciously contrived to give an impression of infinity; here, groupings that focused on extensive vistas were composed according to advanced knowledge of the science of perspective. In the hangar at Orly the elliptical forms of the many adjoining structural segments lend a certain measurelessness to the total effect.

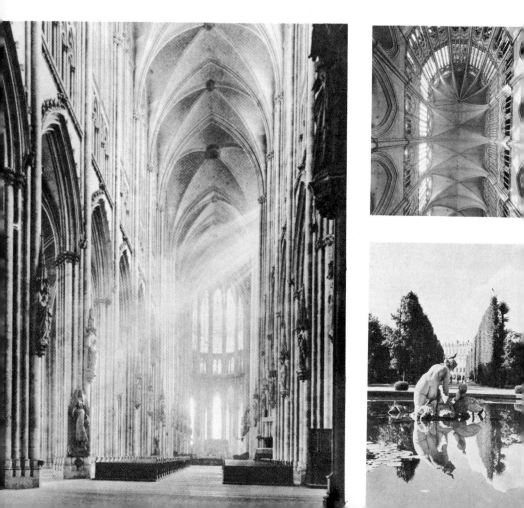

ABOVE: Hangar: Orly, Paris, France, 1925, Eugene Freyssinet, engineer.

FAR LEFT: Cathedral, Interior: Cologne, Germany, 14th to 15th centuries, Gerardus, Arnoldus von Buren, von Falkenberg, and others, architects.

CENTER TOP: Notre Dame Cathedral, Ceiling: Amiens, France, 13th century, Robert de Luzarches, architect. (*Clarence Ward*)

CENTER BOTTOM: Schönbrunn Park: Vienna, Austria, c. 1700, Johann Bernard Fischer von Erlach, architect. (*Fritz Henle*)

BELOW: Notre Dame Cathedral, Triforium: Amiens, France, 13th century, Robert de Luzarches, architect. (*Service Commercial Monuments Historiques*)

Diverse architectural treatments of long passageways emphasize or modulate their inherent perspective quality

The recession of repetitive elements characteristic of one-point perspective is spatially enriched when opposite walls contrast with each other—flat or solid against rhythmical or perforated. Spatial interest is further augmented when simple rhythmical treatment of ceilings contrasts with a more complex rhythmical treatment of the walls.

ABOVE LEFT: Certosa di Pavia: Pavia, Italy, 15th century, Giovanni Galeazzo Visconti, architect.

ABOVE RIGHT: Château d'O: Normandy, France, 18th century. (*Helio Berthaud*)

ABOVE: The Chase Manhattan Bank: New York, New York, United States, 1960, Skidmore, Owings, and Merrill, architects. (*Alexandre Georges*)

BELOW: Chiostro dei Benefattori, Monte Cassino: Cassino, Italy, c. 1600. (*STA Foto*)

Extreme vertical treatment, culminating in bursts of light, etc.

The effect of uninterrupted vertical strips of metal or stone, used to frame and divide windows, is expressively corroborated when the vertical lines are crowned at a brightly illuminated opening. An analogous spatial effect is attained by opposite means when a fountain is set at the base of a vertically regulated structure.

ABOVE: Marienkirche: Stralsund, Germany, c. 14th century. (A. Renger-Patzsch)

RIGHT: Seagram Building: New York, New York, United States, 1958, Ludwig Mies van der Rohe, architect. (Joseph M. Stout)
LEFT: Mile High Center: Denver, Colorado, United States, 1956, I. M. Pei, architect.

The development of roof gardens as defined architectural space

The spatial quality peculiar to architecturally developed roof gardens derives from the fact that they are designed to relate to the entire firmament. They seem suspended in mid-air, completely dissociated from the surface of the earth, to which most buildings are connected not only physically but also by their design.

RIGHT: Cathedral Roof: Milan, Italy, 1490, Simone da Orsenigo, Marco da Campione, and others, architects. (*Ed. A. Traldi, Milan*)
FAR RIGHT: Unité d'Habitation: Marseilles, France, 1952, Le Corbusier, architect. (*Lucien Hervé*)

BELOW LEFT: Villa Savoye: Poissy, France, 1929, Le Corbusier, architect. (*Lucien Hervé*)
BELOW CENTER AND RIGHT: The Château: Chambord, France, 1535, Pierre Nepveu, architect.

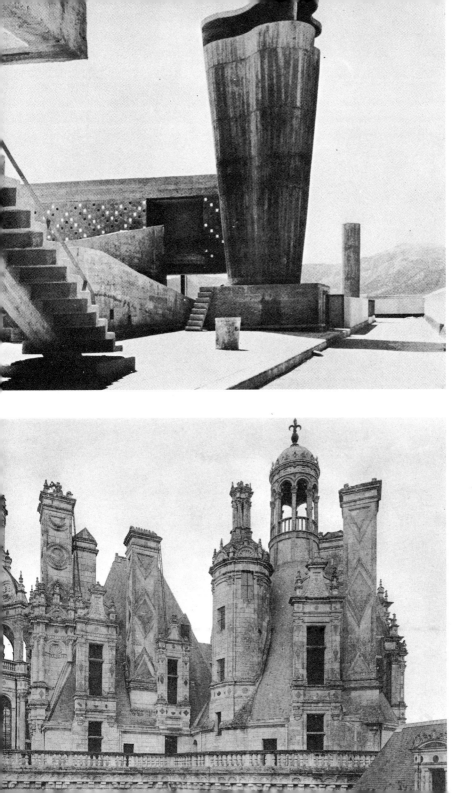

Major Periods of
Western Architecture

Greek—circa 400 B.C.

Characteristic of Greek art and architecture is the development of the concept of three-dimensionality, illustrated by free-standing sculpture and by buildings standing in a free relationship to the landscape. The attempt to express truthfully an inner organization as well as a fully balanced relationship to nature resulted from the Greek interest in rational thinking. This led to a search for a harmonious order in nature and an attempt to relate human experience to it. In classic Greek architecture, for the purpose of achieving a harmonious unity out of many interdependent parts, principles of mathematical order were developed and utilized.

Hellenistic and Roman—150 B.C. to 400 A.D.

Roman architecture was based on Greek classicism; buildings became more highly ornamented, however, as Roman power spread across a far-flung cosmopolitan world. The great public baths, with their elaborate marble facings quite unrelated to the underlying structure, are in keeping with the ostentatious tastes of the Romans. But practical problems of constructing great aqueducts, stadia, public baths led to important engineering advances in the use of the arch and the vault. The latter permitted the development of large and complex interior spaces, which received more attention than in classical Greek architecture. Space rather than form took on importance as a problem in architecture.

Early Christian and Byzantine—5th to 10th Centuries

Early Christian and Byzantine architecture represents a synthesis which incorporated Eastern as well as Greek and Roman influences. The important architecture of this period is primarily religious; after the collapse of the Roman Empire, it reaffirmed in eloquent terms that Christianity was the most prominent influence in the Western world. This period is distinguished from that of classical antiquity by the evolution of the concept of a deep spiritual unity of all mankind. The planar, domed, and vaulted surfaces of the interiors of such buildings as S. Vitale in Ravenna, an important extant example of Byzantine architecture, are covered with shimmering mosaics, fantastically abstract frescoes, and curiously conceived sculptured ornamentation. But these rich interiors are housed in simple, straightforward structures with essentially unadorned exteriors that suggest indifference to outward display and to matters pertaining to this world.

Romanesque and Early Gothic—9th to 12th Centuries

A distinctive quality of early Romanesque architecture is its directness and general lack of embellishment. This was perhaps induced by religious asceticism. Knowledge and culture during this period were largely sustained and controlled by the Church, but there existed a spirit of experimentation in dealing with problems of form, surface, and space which derived from many influences, such as the Arabic, Byzantine, and Nordic.

Romanesque work shares with Byzantine the concern with a vision of a higher spiritual order, but differs from it architecturally. There were two distinct developments in church architecture. The first was an increased emphasis on directional and rhythmical arrangements, through which a progression toward the altar was developed. In Romanesque and later architecture these arrangements determined both the exterior treatment of buildings, where towers became part of the composition, and the interior treatment, where linear motifs gave increased stress on verticality. A dynamic element in design suggests a quest for sublimation, as in the cathedral at Worms. The second development of this period involved a struggle to dematerialize the bodily structure of an edifice by exploiting the structural potentialities of ribbed members whose original function had been the bounding and subdivision of areas. The consequent lessening of actual wall space led to a lighter and much more fluid type of architecture which we know as Gothic.

Gothic—13th to 15th Centuries

The pointed arch, characteristic of Gothic architecture, originated in the East, but Gothic builders rejected other Eastern forms, such as the dome, and circular buildings in general; they preferred a linear and polygonal treatment which would fit into a geometric modular system applicable to groined vaults and other basic techniques of Gothic architecture. The combination of scholastic rationalism and northern pagan traditions developed into a culture independent of the Mediterranean. Only Rome repudiated both this culture and the Gothic style.

The High Gothic system in architecture reached a balanced and unified perfection, exemplified in such inspired structures as the cathedral at Amiens. Its ultimate execution owed much to the well organized, competent medieval building trade groups who played an important role in the commercial centers of northern Europe and were well versed in geometric number relationships and in engineering skills. They set up strict standards and working agreements in general accord with the medieval hierarchical tradition.

As the Gothic style developed a fresh enthusiasm for the concept that basic harmony and vitality can be found in the world, the sculpture and architectural ornamentation of the period, such as the gargoyles of Notre Dame in Paris, became increasingly realistic in form while expressing, frequently at the same time, deep esoteric meanings.

Renaissance—15th and 16th Centuries

During this period the architectural guilds of the Middle Ages were gradually replaced by individual architects, and architecture, like painting, became a liberal art. "Knowledge" came to mean the study of classical antiquity, which was interpreted quite freely. Buildings by different artists were easily identifiable until later, when academic rules for design became more rigid. In the early period of the Renaissance, clarity of form and balanced proportions were favored, in contrast to the complex designs of Gothic buildings. Mathematical relationships were employed to establish an orderly and harmonious equilibrium. The preference for symmetry and for pure forms such as squares, cubes, and spheres was manifested by designs of the period for ideal towns. In accordance with this rational approach to problems of design, perspective was studied, so that in architecture as in painting a reasonable rather than an arbitrary arrangement of objects could be established.

Baroque and Rococo—17th and 18th Centuries

Baroque architecture developed from the architecture of the High Renaissance. The academic rules governing the use of classical orders (Doric, Ionic, Corinthian), followed by Bramante and established earlier on the basis of archaeological studies, were largely disregarded. Classical elements were freely adapted to develop the sculptural potentialities of undulating masses and complex spatial arrangements. The Rococo style, a lighter, more delicate offshoot of this free and partly asymmetrical treatment of form, developed a singularly ornamental fluidity. Creative and imaginative powers of the artist and the architect were encouraged under the patronage of both the clergy and the state. Enormous, ornately furnished palaces and châteaux surrounded by extensive gardens were built by monarchs and imitated by an extravagant European aristocracy. The most famous single example is the 17th-century château of Louis XIV at Versailles.

However, widespread resistance to the stress on grandeur developed in the largely Protestant north. In England, during the 17th century, Sir Christopher Wren emerged as the outstanding architect of his time, and his simple, graceful designs were widely copied and adapted both in his own country and in America. During the second half of the 18th century, through the work of Robert Adam and through new emphasis on the decorative possibilities of the classicistic idiom, the English Rococo style acquired its distinctive qualities.

Neo-Classicism and Romanticism—circa 1800

Toward the end of the 18th century and at the turn of the 19th a new movement—a form of romanticism emphasizing the beauties of Greek antiquity—was reflected in the literature, art, and architecture of the period. The intricate elegance of the rococo, although itself romantic, was associated with the old aristocratic order and was therefore rejected in the late 18th century in favor of buildings of more simple outline. Neo-Classicism was a strong influence even under Napoleon, during the so-called "Empire" period, and flourished throughout Europe, in England, and in America, along with emerging ideas of democracy. But a romantic return to forms of medievalism appeared early in the 19th century.

Residential architecture was predominantly conservative in character; yet a romantic nostalgia for the Middle Ages as well as for the ancient Greeks had such singular repercussions in architecture as, for instance, the use of imitation ruins in landscape design. The same theme was popular in painting and in the interior decoration of large houses.

About the same time the developing industrial revolution encouraged the breaking of rigid academic formulas and the beginning of experimentation, often mechanistic, that presaged late 19th- and early 20th-century developments. This is reflected in the work of the French architect Claude-Nicolas Ledoux.

Modern—19th and 20th Centuries

In the architecture of the second half of the 19th century there is evidence of a reaction against any specific order or uniformity. A proliferation of imitations of historical styles reflected the notion of laissez faire. The unassimilated ideas of romanticism, eclecticism, and materialism only confused the issue, since most of these ideas were literary and therefore hard to translate into the idiom of architecture, in which problems of expression in form, space, texture, line, and color take precedence. Ideas associated with utilitarianism encouraged the operations of builders who laid little stress on aesthetic criteria, with deplorable results as far as much of the domestic architecture was concerned.

Recognition of the gap between literary ideas and architectural techniques led to the English arts and crafts movement, which affirmed that a relationship between the maker and the finished product was necessary for the creation of objects more beautiful and significant in form than machine-made products. This movement, to a limited extent, spread over Europe. In the meantime, the work of engineers dealing with new utilitarian requirements and new materials resulted in structures that demonstrated new possibilities in building. Most academically trained architects, both in Europe and in America, were designing façades that were incongruous when supported by steel or concrete skeleton construction. But around 1900 in Chicago, where academic traditions were weaker than they were elsewhere, some architects attempted to solve this problem by working on the premise that form should follow function. In Germany, about the same time, it was realized that the arts and crafts movement would be unable to progress unless integrated with the new industrial developments. The *Deutsche Werkbund* was founded, and under its direction an effort was made to find suitable and gratifying forms that might be the logical outcome of a mechanical process of production. A new analysis of basic principles in relation to problems of form, however, had its roots in the arts and crafts movement. Many experiments by architects in various parts of the Western world finally pointed toward a more cohesive approach—partly the result of recognition of the characteristics of steel and concrete construction and partly inspired by the work of abstract painters and sculptors. Aesthetically, architects are in debt to the artists' interpretation of a scientific era. Sociologists and other scientific workers, involved in extensive research, have been contributing to understanding of the relationship between various types of housing facilities and other urban amenities, such as schools and shopping centers. Through such investigations, new forms in architecture continue to evolve. The more successful designs are arrived at by a process of integration as well as by an imaginative interpretation of the changing perspectives.

Bibliography

Bauhaus: Weimar, 1919–25, Dessau, 1925–28. Boston: Charles T. Branford, 1952. London: Bailey and Swinfen, 1952.

BAUMER, FRANKLIN LE VAN (ed). *Main Currents of Western Thought.* New York: Alfred A. Knopf, 1952.

BEHRENDT, WALTER CURT. *Modern Building.* New York: Harcourt, Brace and Company, 1937. London: Martin Hopkinson, 1938.

BENEDICT, RUTH. *Patterns of Culture.* New York: New American Library of World Literature. London: Routledge and Kegan Paul, 1935.

BRAUN, JULIE. *Art, the Image of the West.* New York: Pantheon Books, 1952.

BRINTON, CRANE. *Ideas and Men: The Story of Western Thought.* New York: Prentice-Hall, 1950. London: Jonathan Cape, 1951.

CASSOU, JEAN; LANGUI, EMIL; and PEVSNER, NIKOLAUS. *Gateway to the Twentieth Century.* New York: McGraw-Hill Book Company, 1962. *The Sources of Modern Art.* London: Thames and Hudson, 1962.

CORBUSIER, LE. *Towards a New Architecture.* New York: Harcourt, Brace and Company, 1927. London: Architectural Press, 1947.

DEWEY, JOHN. *Art as Experience.* New York: Minton, Balch and Company, 1934. London: G. Allen and Unwin, 1934.

DORNER, ALEXANDER. *The Way beyond Art: The Work of Herbert Bayer.* New York: Wittenborn, Schultz, Inc., 1947.

FRIEDRICH, CARL J. *The Age of the Baroque.* New York: Harper and Brothers, 1952. London: Hamish Hamilton, 1952.

GARDNER, PERCY. *Principles of Greek Art.* New York: The Macmillan Company, 1914. London: Macmillan and Co., 1914.

GIEDION, SIGFRIED. *Mechanization Takes Command.* Toronto: Oxford University Press, 1948.

———. *Space, Time, and Architecture.* Cambridge, Mass.: Harvard University Press, 1941.

GROPIUS, WALTER. *The New Architecture and the Bauhaus.* London: Faber and Faber, 1955.

KANDINSKY, WASSILY. *Point and Line to Plane.* New York: Solomon Guggenheim Foundation, 1947.

KLEE, PAUL. *On Modern Art*. London: Faber and Faber, 1948.

LAMONT, CORLISS. *Humanism as a Philosophy*. New York: Philosophical Library, 1949.

MUMFORD, LEWIS (ed.). *Roots of Contemporary American Architecture*. New York: Reinhold Publishing Corporation, 1952. London: Chapman and Hall, 1952.

PANOFSKY, ERWIN. *Gothic Architecture and Scholasticism*. Latrobe, Pa.: Archabbey Press, 1951.

—— (ed. and tr.). *Abbot Suger on the Abbey Church of St-Denis and Its Art Treasures*. Princeton: Princeton University Press, 1946.

PEVSNER, NIKOLAUS. *An Outline of European Architecture*. Baltimore: Penguin Books, 1960. Harmondsworth: Penguin Books, 1960.

——. *Pioneers of Modern Design*. New York: Museum of Modern Art, 1949. London: Faber and Faber, 1936.

READ, HERBERT E. *Art and Society*. London: Faber and Faber, 1945.

RICHTER, GISELA M. A. *The Sculpture and Sculptors of the Greeks*. New Haven: Yale University Press, 1950. London: Oxford University Press, 1951.

RUSSELL, BERTRAND. *A History of Western Philosophy*. New York: Simon and Schuster, 1945. London: Allen and Unwin, 1946.

SCOTT, GEOFFREY. *The Architecture of Humanism*. New York: Charles Scribner's Sons, 1924. London: Constable and Co., 1924.

SULLIVAN, LOUIS H. *Kindergarten Chats on Architecture, Education, and Democracy*. Washington, D. C.: Scarab Fraternity Press, 1934.

WHITEHEAD, A. N. *Science and the Modern World*. New York: New American Library of World Literature, 1956. Cambridge: Cambridge University Press, 1936.

WITTKOWER, RUDOLF. *Architectural Principles in the Age of Humanism*. London: Alec Tiranti, Ltd., 1952.

WORRINGER, WILHELM. *Form Problems of Gothic*. New York: G. E. Stechert and Company, 1920. *Form in Gothic*. London: Putnam and Sons, 1927.

WRIGHT, FRANK LLOYD. *Selected Writings, 1894–1940*. New York: Duell, Sloan and Pearce, 1941.

Photographic Sources

page

14–15 Weissenhof Housing, Stuttgart: *Bau und Wohnung* (1927) Karl Kramer Verlag, Stuttgart, and Akademischer Verlag Dr. Wedekind.

22–23 Chemical Factory, Luban: *Bauten der Technik* by W. Lindner, Verlag Ernst Wasmuth, Tübingen, West Germany, 1927.

22–23 Trinita di Delia, Castelvetrano, and S. Giovanni degli Eremiti, Palermo, Sicily: *L'architettura Arabo-Normanna e il Rinacimento in Sicilia* by Giulio V. Arata, Bestetti e Tumminelli, Editori d'Arte, Milan, 1924.

24–25 Hohenstaufen Palace, Wimpfen, Germany: Hans Knöpfel Verlag, N. Heilbronn.

24–25 Steiner House, Vienna: *Adolf Loos, das Werk des Architecten* by Heinrich Kulka, Buch- und Kunstverlag Anton Schroll and Co., Vienna, 1931.

24–25 Tramway Workers' Club, Moscow: *Russland* by El. Lissitzky, Buch- und Kunstverlag Anton Schroll and Co., Vienna, 1930.

24–25 Yselmonde Railroad Signal Box, Utrecht: *Die neue Baukunst* by Bruno Taut, Julius Hoffmann Verlag, Stuttgart, 1929.

26–27 Turbinenfabrik-A.E.G., Berlin: *Peter Behrens* by P. J. Cremers, G. D. Baedeker Verlag, Essen, 1928.

26–27 Bauhaus, Dessau: *A History of Modern Architecture* by J. Joedicke, Frederick A. Praeger, Inc., New York, 1959.

28–29 I.I.T. Boiler Plant, Chicago: *Postwar Architecture* by Henry-Russell Hitchcock and Arthur Drexler, Museum of Modern Art, New York, 1952.

28–29 Chrysler Corporation Truck Plant Ex-

port Building: *Industrial Architecture* by Albert Kahn, Inc., George Nelson, 1939.

30–31 Artisan's Atelier, France, and Salt Granary, Compiègne: *Ledoux Architecte du Roi* by Raval and Moreux.

32–33 Village Hall, Saynatsalo, Finland: *Alvar Aalto* by Frederick Gutheim, George Braziller, Inc., New York, 1960.

34–35 Schröder House, Utrecht: *De Stijl 1917–31* by H. L. C. Jaffe, Alec Tiranti, Ltd., London, 1956.

34–35 Schlosshof in Alten Schloss: Verlag von Gustav Haufler, Stuttgart.

40–41 Chiesa di S. Andrea del Quirinale, Rome: *Il Barocco a Roma* by Giulio Magni, C. Crudo and C., Societa Italiana di Edizioni Artistiche, 1911.

40–41 Château de Josselin, Brittany: *Châteaux de France Anciens et Modernes* by Hector St. Sauveuri, C. J. Massin Éditeur, Paris.

40–41 Lenin Institute, Moscow: *Russland* by El. Lissitzky, Buch- und Kunstverlag Anton Schroll and Co., Vienna, 1930.

42–43 Werkbund Exposition Building, Cologne: *Walter Gropius* by J. M. Fitch, George Braziller, Inc., New York.

44–45 Neubuhl Housing, Zurich: *Documents d'Urbanisme* by R. Auzelle, Éditions Vincent, Freal et Cie., Paris, 1952.

44–45 Haarlem Terrace, The Netherlands: G. L. Burke, *The Making of Dutch Towns*, Cleaver-Hume Press, Ltd., London, 1956.

44–45 Dwelling—Central Area, Lübeck, and Drawing: K. Gruber, *Die Gestalt der deutschen Stadt*, Verlag Georg D. W. Callwey, Munich.

80–81 Mosse Pavilion of Pressa, Cologne: *Glas im Bau* by Arthur Korn, Ernst Pollak Verlag, Berlin, 1929.

82–83 Monument, Moscow: *Russland* by El. Lissitzky, Buch- und Kunstverlag von Anton Schroll and Co., Vienna, 1930.

82–83 S. Andrea della Fratte, Rome: *Il Barocco a Roma* by Giulio Magni, C. Crudo and C., Societa Italiana di Edizioni Artistiche, 1911.

86–87 Wohnhauser der "Gehag," Berlin: *Die neue Baukunst* by Bruno Taut, Julius Hoffmann Verlag, Stuttgart, 1929.

88–89 Pitti Palace, Florence: *Palast Architektur von Ober-Italien* by Dr. A. Haupt, Verlag Ernst Wasmuth, Tübingen, West Germany, 1922.

90–91 Corn Silo, South America: *International Architecture* by Walter Gropius, Albert Langen Verlag, Munich, 1925.

90–91 Bauhaus, Dessau: *A History of Modern Architecture* by J. Joedicke, Frederick A. Praeger, Inc., New York, 1959.

90–91 Fisher Body Co., Cleveland: *Industrial and Commercial Buildings* by Albert Kahn, Inc., 1925.

90–91 A.E.G., Berlin: *International Architecture* by Walter Gropius, Albert Langen Verlag, Munich, 1925.

94–95 Berlin Remodeling: *Mies van der Rohe* by L. Hilbersheimer, published by Paul Theobold and Company, Chicago, 1956.

94–95 Grottanelli Palace, Siena: *Palast Architektur von Ober-Italien* by Dr. A. Haupt, Verlag Ernst Wasmuth, Tübingen, West Germany, 1922.

94–95 Rue de Rivoli, *Paris* by Mario von Bueorich, Albertus Verlag, Berlin, 1928.

96–97 Telschow Building, Berlin: *Glas im Bau* by Arthur Korn, Ernst Pollak Verlag, Berlin, 1929.

100–101 School of Art, Library, Glasgow: *Die neue Baukunst* by Bruno Taut, Julius Hoffmann Verlag, Stuttgart, 1929.

102–103 Eiffel Tower: *Die neue Baukunst* by Bruno Taut, Julius Hoffmann Verlag, Stuttgart, 1929.

102–103 Hôtel de Sens, Paris, University of Michigan, Archives Photographiques d'art et d'histoire.

102–103 Hochzeitsturm, Darmstadt: *A History of Modern Architecture* by J. Joedicke, Frederick A. Praeger, Inc., New York, 1959.

104–105 St. James Square Staircase, London: *The Architecture of Robert and James Adam* by Arthur T. Bolton, Charles Scribner's Sons, New York, 1922.

104–105 Hayward House, Charleston: *Examples of Colonial Architecture in South Carolina and Georgia* by E. A. Crane and E. E. Soderholtz, Bruno Hessling Co., Ltd., New York.

104–105 Villa di Papa Giulio III, Rome: *Il Barocco a Roma* by Giulio Magni, C. Crudo and C., Societa Italiana di Edizioni Artistiche, 1911.

106–107 House, Lake Geneva: *Adolf Loos* by Heinrich Kulka, Buch- und Kunstverlag Anton Schroll and Co., Vienna, 1931.

108–109 Maison du Peuple, Como: *Encyclopédie de l'Architecture Nouvelle, Ordre et Climat Mediterranéens* by Alberto Sartoris, Ulrico Hoepli Éditeur, Milan, 1948.

110–111 Fleischalle, Haarlem: *Architectur und Kunstgewerbe in Alt-Holland* by Jan Lauweriks, Delphin Verlag, Munich, 1924.

110–111 Little Moreton Hall, Cheshire: *English Homes* by H. Avray Tipping, Charles Scribner's Sons, New York.

112–113 S. Maria la Nuova, Monreale: *L'architecttura Arabo-Normanna e il Rinascimento in Sicilia* by Giulio V. Arata, Bestetti e Tumminelli, Editori d'Arte, Milan, 1924.

112–113 Soane's House, London: *Sir John Soane* by J. N. Summerson, Art and Technics, Ltd., London, 1952.

114–115 Porta Aurea in Diocletian's Palace, Split: *Denkmaeler der Kunst in Dalmatien* by George Kowalczyk, Verlag von Franz Malota, Vienna, 1910.

114–115 Thannhauser Art Gallery, Berlin: *Glas im Bau* by Arthur Korn, Ernst Pollak Verlag, Berlin, 1929.

116–117 Cathedral, Murcia: *Was ist Barock?* By Dr. Ludwig Lang, Montana Verlag A.G., Zurich, Ruschlikon, and Stuttgart.

116–117 Department Store, Berlin: *Plastik und Raum als Grundformen künstlerischer Gestaltung*, by A. E. Brinkmann, Piper, Munich, 1922.

L'arte Bizantina in Italia by A. Colasanti, Bestetti e Tumminelli Editori d'arte, Milan.

158–159 I. G. Farben, Höchst am Main: *Peter Behrens* by P. J. Cremers, G. D. Baedeker Verlag, Essen, 1928.

160–161 Schönbrunn Palace, Vienna: Echte Fotografiekarten Industrie A.G., Vienna.

160–161 Rathaus, Lüneburg: *Deutsche Baukunst des Mittelalters und der Renaissance,* Verlagsarchiv Karl Robert Langewiesche Nachfolger Hans Köster, Königstein im Taunus, 1920.

164–165 Cathedral, Strasbourg: *Das Strassburger Münster* by G. Dehio, Piper, Munich, 1922.

166–167 Metal Workers' Union, Berlin: *Eric Mendelsohn* by Arnold Whittick, Leonard Hill Books, Ltd., London, 1956.

166–167 Double Stair, Graz: Photographie und Verlag, Photo Kopieranstalt, Fritz Grafl, Graz.

166–167 Barberini Palace, Rome: *Il Barocco a Roma* by Giulio Magni, C. Crudo and C., Societa Italiana de Edizioni Artistiche, 1911.

168–169 Schloss Brühl: *Was ist Barock?* by Dr. Ludwig Lang, Montana Verlag A.G., Zurich, Ruschlikon, and Stuttgart.

170–171 Mosque, Córdoba: *History of Spanish Architecture* by Bernard Beven, Charles Scribner's Sons, New York, 1939.

172–173 Cathedral interior, Cologne: *German Cathedrals* by Julius Baum, The Vanguard Press, New York, 1956.

172–173 Hangar, Orly: *Bauten der Technik* by W. Lindner, Verlag Ernst Wasmuth, Tübingen, West Germany, 1927.

172–173 Notre Dame Cathedral, Ceiling, Amiens: *A History of Western Art* by J. I. Sewall, Holt, Rinehart and Winston, Inc., New York, 1953.

Index